URUGUAY

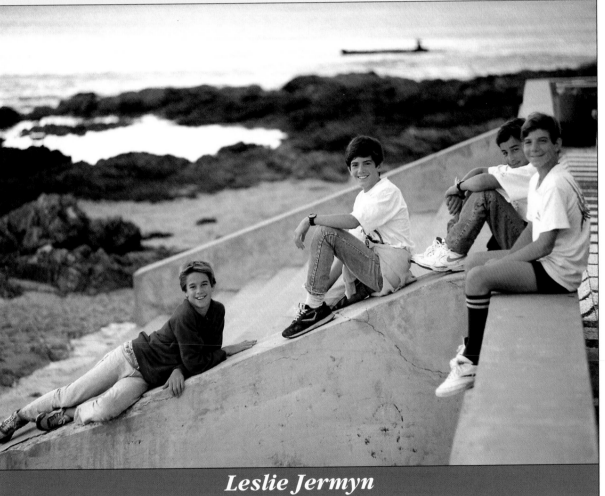

Leslie Jermyn

MARSHALL CAVENDISH
New York • London • Sydney

Reference edition published 1999 by
Marshall Cavendish Corporation
99 White Plains Road
Tarrytown
New York 10591

© Times Editions Pte Ltd 1999

Originated and designed by
Times Books International, an imprint of
Times Editions Pte Ltd

Printed in Malaysia

Library of Congress Cataloging-in-Publication Data:

Jermyn, Leslie.
    Uruguay / Leslie Jermyn.
        p. cm.—(Cultures of the World)
    Includes bibliographical references and index.
    Summary: Describes the geography, history, government,
economy, people, lifestyle, religion, language, arts, leisure,
festivals, and food of the smallest country in South America.
    ISBN 0-7614-0873-8 (library binding)
    1. Uruguay—Juvenile literature. [1. Uruguay] I. Title.
II. Series.
F2708.5.J47   1999
989.5—dc21   98–27375
                        CIP
                        AC

INTRODUCTION

URUGUAY IS A TINY country sandwiched between the giants of Argentina and Brazil. It is distinguished as a country that has long supported the ideals of free speech, democracy, and equality. The country has few natural resources, but extremes of poverty and wealth are not as pronounced here as in other places on the continent. The early and tragic disappearance of native peoples left behind a nearly homogeneous group of descendants of European settlers. Uruguay has long been a trading nation, exchanging people and ideas along with goods, and has produced a disproportionate number of writers and artists for its tiny population. This small republic was terrorized during a military dictatorship that lasted 12 long and painful years. Since the return to democracy in 1985, Uruguayans have faced the challenge of rebuilding their country in a changing world economy. But Uruguayans are committed to maintaining their ideals of freedom and social welfare, whatever the cost.

CONTENTS

Mate (**"MAH-tay"**) cups and *bombillas* (**"bohm-BEEL-ya"**), or straws, are an important part of Uruguayan life.

CONTENTS

The sereina: just one of the many beautiful birds that can be found in the Uruguayan grasslands.

GEOGRAPHY

URUGUAY, officially La República Oriental del Uruguay, is a small country located in South America on the Atlantic seaboard, sandwiched between the two largest countries of that continent: Brazil to the north and Argentina to the west and south. It covers an area of about 68,020 square miles (176,220 square km) and is about the same size as North Dakota. The capital city, Montevideo, is in the south of the country on the Río de la Plata (Silver River).

The perimeter of Uruguay is 1,147 miles (1,846 km) long, and all but 175 miles (282 km) is made up of waterways or ocean. To the south is the Río de la Plata estuary where the Río Uruguay empties into the Atlantic Ocean. The Río Uruguay separates Uruguay from Argentina on the west and the Merín Lagoon marks the border with Brazil in the northeast. In the north, Uruguay and Brazil are separated by the Río Cuareim. The most important river is the Río Negro or Black River, which flows from northeast to southwest across the country.

A dam built on the Río Negro has created the largest artificial lake in South America, Black River Lake.

Left: **In the low and rolling hills of the Cuchilla Grande, looking to the north.**

Opposite: **An old pier on the Río de la Plata in Colonia.**

Playa Mansa or Mansa Beach at Punta del Este, a favorite vacation destination of Uruguayans.

URUGUAY'S REGIONS

Uruguay is made up of gently rolling plains with no hills over 2,000 feet (610 m) above sea level. There are two ridges of hills in the north and east of the country called Cuchilla de Haedo and Cuchilla Grande where Mount Catedral, the country's highest point, can be found. Although there are no dramatic differences in geography across the country, there are three regions that differ in human settlement patterns and land use: the interior to the north, the Atlantic seaboard to the east, and the littoral or shore of the Río de la Plata and the Río Uruguay to the south and west.

THE INTERIOR This is the largest region and it includes most of the central portion of the country. It is mainly grassland with very little forest. Only 2–3% of the country is forested. These wooded areas, called gallery forests, grow along the edges of rivers. The soil of this area is not very rich and therefore does not support intensive agriculture. Most of this land is used for raising cattle and sheep on large ranches.

Feet		Meters
16,500		5,000
9,900		3,000
6,600		2,000
3,300		1,000
1,650		500
660		200
0		0

N

0   50   100 Miles
0   50   100   150 Kilometers

ARTIGAS

Río Cuareim

Cuchilla de Belén

Salto Grande

SALTO

RIVERA

BRAZIL

ARGENTINA

PAYSANDÚ

TACUAREMBÓ

Cuchilla de Haedo

Río Negro

CERRO LARGO

RÍO NEGRO

Río Negro (Black R.)

Black River Lake

DURAZNO

TREINTA Y TRES

Río Yi

Merín Lagoon

Río Uruguay

Río Y

SORIANO   FLORES

LAVALLEJA

FLORIDA

COLONIA

SAN JOSÉ

Río Santa Lucia

ROCHA

Mt. Catedral (1,684ft/513m)

CANELONES   MALDONADO

MONTEVIDEO   ▲ Mt. Animas

Río de la Plata (Silver River)

ATLANTIC

OCEAN

The alluvial soil of the littoral, which is enriched by the periodic flooding of the rivers, is the country's most arable land.

THE ATLANTIC SEABOARD This is the band of land that stretches east from Montevideo and then north toward Brazil along the Atlantic Ocean. Close to Montevideo, the coastline is sandy and dotted with vacation resorts and small settlements of people who commute to Montevideo to work. The shore turns north at Punta del Este or East Point. This is the biggest vacation resort in Uruguay.

THE LITTORAL This area consists of the shores of the Río de la Plata and the Río Uruguay to the west and north of Montevideo. Most of Uruguay's food crops are grown in this area and a bridge across the Uruguay River at Paysandú makes trade with Argentina very easy. Most Uruguayans live in this region—in Montevideo, Canelones, and Salto. The greater Montevideo area, Canelones and San José departments, are home to more than half of Uruguay's 3.1 million inhabitants.

CLIMATE

Uruguay lies completely within the temperate zone so the climate is quite moderate with few extremes. There are four distinct seasons, but because Uruguay is south of the equator, the seasons are the reverse of those in North America. January is the middle of summer with temperatures ranging from 63°F to 82°F (17–28°C). July, the height of winter, has average temperatures of 43°F to 57°F (6–14°C). There is no distinct rainy season, though there is slightly more rainfall in the winter. Since there are no mountains, rain falls fairly evenly across the country. Winter and spring are characterized by high winds subject to rapid shifts in direction. With no mountain ranges or other natural barriers to stop them, winds can be violent and sometimes tornadoes develop. Occasionally, cold north winds from the plains of Argentina cause temperatures to drop in the winter, while winds off the Atlantic Ocean in the summer bring cooler temperatures.

Large thistles can be found in the rolling grasslands of the interior.

FLORA AND FAUNA

The gallery forests contain a variety of trees including eucalyptus, willow, poplar, and acacia. One of the strangest trees in the country is the ombú. The bark of this tree appears soft and fluffy. The ceiba tree has beautiful scarlet flowers. There are also palm trees along the southern shore. The rest of the country is covered by grasses and shrubs.

With so much water, both salt and fresh, there is an abundance of marine life. Freshwater fish include the piranha, golden salmon, and pejerrey. There is also pacú, tararira, and surubí, which are similar to North American perch and bass. The most famous of the freshwater fish is the criolla (creole), which can weigh up to 70 pounds (32 kilos). People come from all over the Americas to fish for criolla in the Río Santa Lucía. The Río de la Plata estuary is extremely rich in fauna. The warm ocean currents from Brazil meet with the colder ones from Argentina, giving the estuary a combination of fresh and salt waters. Sharks, rays, anchovies, and corvina can be found in these waters.

The river forests and lagoon marshes are home to dozens of species of birds. Some of the birds that live in wetlands are the royal duck, black-necked swan, creole duck, and various types of wild geese. The grasslands support partridges and the rhea. The *hornero* ("or-NAY-roh") or oven-bird builds oven-shaped nests on fence posts and telephone poles all over the country.

Many of Uruguay's larger mammals, like the jaguar, puma, collared peccary, and giant anteater, are no longer found in Uruguay because of loss of habitat or over-hunting. Among those that remain are the foxes, white-lipped peccaries, armadillos, carpinchos (capybaras), coatimundis, and three-toed anteaters. The Atlantic coast also attracts a large colony of sea lions. They breed on Isla de Lobos, an island near Montevideo, and along the rocky eastern coast.

As ranching expanded throughout Uruguay's interior, open grasslands were fenced in and the animals killed off. Some of the endangered and protected animals today are the caiman (a type of alligator), coatimundi, rhea, flamenco, capybara, creole duck, and black-necked swan.

The armadillo, one of the few indigenous animals that can still be found in Uruguay.

WONDROUS ANIMALS OF URUGUAY

The armadillo is one of the very few mammals that have a protective shell. Its shell is made of strips of hard material called scutes that are joined by flesh. When threatened, the armadillo will roll up in a ball to protect its soft underbelly. It also digs very fast and sometimes digs its way to safety. W.H. Hudson, an English traveler to Uruguay in the 19th century, described the armadillo as a "little old bent-backed gentleman in a rusty black coat trotting briskly about on some very important business." Female armadillos give birth to litters of identical males or females that are like genetic clones.

The tamanduá or three-toed anteater is a smaller cousin of the giant anteater, which is now extinct in Uruguay. The tamanduá spends about half its life in trees and is a very good climber. It has a prehensile tail that can grab and hold on to things like tree branches. Anteaters have large claws on the forefeet for self-defense and for breaking into insect hiding places. They eat only insects but have no teeth to chew them with, so their stomachs grind up the tough outer shells of insects like mixing machines.

The rhea or ñandú is a large ostrich-like bird that stands 5 feet (1.5 m) tall and weighs about 50 pounds (23 kilos). It cannot fly but can run very fast. Rheas live in family groups containing one male and many females. All the females will lay their eggs in one nest for the male to incubate. These birds have long been hunted for their hide and feathers, which are used as dusters.

The capybara (below) is the world's largest rodent. It usually lives near water and its eyes and ears are positioned very high on its head to allow it to swim easily. Its partially webbed feet also help with swimming. This animal has been hunted extensively for its meat.

A view of the Montevideo skyline by night. Cerro de Montevideo or the Montevideo Hill can be seen in the distance.

CITIES

MONTEVIDEO The biggest and most important city is Montevideo, the capital. The population density is almost 4,000 people per square mile (2,500 per square km). Montevideo, with a population of approximately 1.4 million, is home to nearly half the people in Uruguay, making it almost a city-state. It is located across the Río de la Plata from Buenos Aires, Argentina. Both of Uruguay's universities are in Montevideo, as are most of its television, radio, and newspaper companies. This is the seat of government, and more than two-thirds of Uruguay's industry is located in or near the capital.

Montevideo was founded in 1726 on a promontory near a large bay that forms a perfect natural harbor. It has gentle hills sloping to the sea. The main street runs along the back of Cuchilla Grande. Across the bay from the Old City is the Cerro de Montevideo or Montevideo Hill, which gave the city its name. Although this city is the youngest capital in South America, it is considered one of the loveliest.

14

OTHER CITIES AND TOWNS The next largest cities in Uruguay are Salto and Paysandú, both located on the Río Uruguay. These cities have developed as a result of farming and trade with Argentina. Salto has benefited from the construction of a hydroelectric dam just north of the city, while Paysandú was given a huge boost by the construction of the General Artigas Bridge that crosses to Argentina.

The towns of Colonia and Punta del Este are both prime tourist destinations. Colonia was originally founded by the Portuguese settlers in Brazil in 1860 and thus is older than Montevideo. Punta del Este was founded in the 20th century as a resort town and has grown steadily. It attracts many local and foreign tourists during the summer.

WHAT'S IN A NAME?

The first thing in Uruguay named by Europeans was the wide estuary where some of South America's major rivers drain into the Atlantic. This was inappropriately called the Río de la Plata (River of Silver) by the first explorers in 1500. There was no silver in the area so historians speculate that the Spaniards named the river in hopes that it would lead to riches in the interior. When Spain established a colony in present-day Buenos Aires, they named the area of Argentina, Uruguay, and Paraguay, the Viceroyalty of Río Plata. During the colonial period, present-day Uruguay was known as the *Banda Oriental* or the East Bank because of its location east of the estuary. For a brief five-year period (1820–25), Brazil controlled Uruguay and called it Cisplatine Province. Finally, in 1828, Uruguay gained its independence from Buenos Aires, Brazil, and Spain, and took the name República Oriental del Uruguay. The name Uruguay comes from the indigenous Guaraní language and means "the river where the birds live."

Montevideo was named by one of Ferdinand Magellan's crew in 1520. As they were sailing up the estuary, the lookout saw the conical hill of Montevideo and cried out "*Monte vide eu*" (I see a mountain). During the 19th century, two factions fought for control of the new country. For 12 years (1838–51), one group laid siege to the city, while the other defended it. During the war and afterwards, Montevideo was known as the "Modern Troy" because, like Troy of ancient Greece, it was forced to defend itself in a civil war.

HISTORY

THE HISTORY OF URUGUAY has been affected by its geographic position between Argentina and Brazil. Nevertheless, Uruguay has maintained a distinct identity and for most of the 20th century has achieved unparalleled levels of education and well-being for its citizens. This chapter describes how the country has handled foreign relations and self-direction.

URUGUAY BEFORE THE SPANISH

Today, Uruguay is the only country in South America that has no surviving indigenous people. The first archeological evidence of human settlement in the area that was to become Uruguay is 8,000 years old. These earliest settlers hunted animals and gathered plant and animal resources in order to survive. From around 4,000 to 8,000 years ago, the stone tools these hunter-gatherers used became more sophisticated and they developed the use of the bow and arrow. By 2,000 years ago, archeological evidence suggests the existence of three distinct groups—the Chaná, Guaraní, and Charrúa—and these were all present at the time of the first European discovery of the territory in the 1500s.

THE CHANÁ were hunter-gatherers who supplemented their diet with fishing. They used the bow and arrow, and they smoked fish to preserve it. They traveled in small groups and were highly nomadic. Not much is known of these people because they disappeared soon after the Spaniards started to settle in Uruguay.

THE GUARANÍ also disappeared quickly from this area, but much more is known about their way of life because they are a large cultural group that still exists in other parts of South America. The Guaraní were shifting cultivators. They planted crops in small garden plots in the forest and they would periodically shift to avoid depleting the soil. They also hunted and

The Guaraní grew corn, beans, cotton, and yerba mate ("YAYR-bah MAH-tay"). Mate, a tea derived from this plant, and a stimulant that contains caffeine, was later adopted into the European culture of Uruguay.

gathered to supplement their diet. They arrived in the area of the Río de la Plata about 200 years before the Europeans, but few survived the first European settlement.

THE CHARRÚA were hunter-gatherers who used the bow and arrow. Unlike the Chaná, however, some of these people survived into the 19th century and played an important role in the wars of independence from Spain. One of their most enduring legacies are *bolas* or *boleadoras* ("boh-lay-ah-DOR-ahs"), a weapon made of rocks attached by long, leather thongs. The hunter swings the *bolas* around over his head and then throws them spinning through the air to wrap around the neck or legs of the

"The Last of the Char-rúas," a sculpture in a park in Montevideo.

hunted animal. The rocks would either kill the animal outright or at least hobble it. This weapon was adopted later by the Spaniards for rounding up horses and cattle on the open plains. The Charrúa were able hunters and fighters and managed to survive in part by hunting the cattle introduced by the Spaniards in the 1600s. The last band of Charrúas was decimated at the Massacre of Salsipuedes.

DISAPPEARANCE OF THE NATIVE POPULATION It is estimated that there were about 9,000 Charrúa and 6,000 Chaná and Guaraní at the time of contact with Europeans in the 1500s. By the time of independence, some 300 years later, there were only about 500 native peoples remaining in Uruguay. There were three main causes for the disintegration and disappearance of native cultures: disease, intentional extermination, and assimilation.

In the late 1500s and early 1600s, Europeans believed that the indigenous peoples of the New World were not fully human. They therefore set out to kill or enslave them. The native people of Uruguay were generally good fighters and much more effective with their lances and arrows than the Spaniards were with their short-range, inaccurate guns. The cause of most of the decline in native populations was disease. Europeans brought many new diseases to the New World including influenza, syphilis, tuberculosis, and smallpox. With no immunity to these diseases, native peoples were quickly decimated.

Finally, some native groups were forced into settlements run by religious groups. The goal of the priests was to convert the natives to Catholicism and change their way of life. As most of Uruguay's native peoples were nomadic, they rarely stayed long in these settlements, but in a sense, this just made them more vulnerable to being hunted down by other Spaniards.

The decline of the natives through diseases brought by Europeans is still continuing today as the few remaining indigenous groups of the Amazon jungle come into contact with non-native peoples.

EUROPEAN DISCOVERY AND SETTLEMENT (1502–1810)

As early as 1502, Europeans had sighted Río de la Plata but did not explore it further. Then in 1516, Juan Díaz de Solís led a Spanish expedition up the estuary. They thought they had found the tip of South America when they landed about 70 miles (113 km) east of modern Montevideo. The landing party was killed instantly by Charrúas and the remaining crew abandoned the site. The Spaniards attempted to found settlements along various rivers throughout the 1500s but were repeatedly repelled by Indian attack.

In 1580, they established a foothold with the second founding of Buenos Aires. In 1603, Governor Hernando Arias of Ascunción ordered that cattle and horses be released into the grasslands of Uruguay. The animals multiplied and attracted Buenos Aires ranchers, who crossed the river to capture the herds; but they never settled permanently on the Uruguayan side.

The Portuguese were the first people to be successful in settling Uruguay. They founded the city of Colonia directly opposite Buenos Aires in 1680. In response to this, the Spaniards founded Montevideo farther east along the estuary in 1726.

INDEPENDENCE (1810–28)

The hero of the story of Uruguayan independence is José Gervasio Artigas (1764–1850). He was the first to organize an army whose purpose was to free Uruguay from Spain, Buenos Aires, and Brazilian interests. In 1810, fighting started in Buenos Aires between two factions: those who wanted Buenos Aires and all of Río de la Plata to separate from Spain against those who wanted to remain loyal to the Spanish crown.

Artigas led the fight against the Spaniards with a ragtag band of Indians and ranchers. They successfully expelled the Spanish governor from Montevideo in 1814. But Brazil, seeing that the newly liberated territory was weakened by the revolution, decided to invade. In 1816 Artigas managed to repel a Brazilian attack, but by 1820, the Brazilians defeated him. They exiled Artigas and called their new territory Cisplatine Province.

Opposite: **The lighthouse at Colonia, a city founded by the Portuguese that predates Montevideo.**

Left: **The fort of General Artigas on Montevideo Hill.**

The fighting stopped for five years during which time the British traded freely with the Brazilians for hides. In 1825 a group of 33 exiles from Montevideo led by Juan Antonio Lavalleja and aided by Argentina, invaded Cisplatine, and fighting started again. With renewed hostilities, the British could not trade in the area and so decided to intervene diplomatically. The Brazilians and the Argentinians, with the help of British diplomacy, finally agreed to the establishment of an independent country between them. This buffer state became known as the República Oriental del Uruguay and was granted its freedom in 1828. Lavalleja's group became known as the "Immortal 33" for their part in aiding the cause of Uruguayan freedom.

ARTIGAS: URUGUAY'S WASHINGTON

José Gervasio Artigas was born in Montevideo in 1764. His family was prominent and wealthy and he was educated by Franciscan friars. His experiences working with the gaucho, or the low-class cowboys, taught him to love the countryside and the common people. He was appointed head of the local Montevideo militia in 1799 and was quick to join the fighting when the first independence movement started in Buenos Aires in 1810. He had his first military success against the forces loyal to Spain in 1811 at the Battle of Las Piedras. When a peace agreement was reached between independence fighters and Spanish loyalists in 1811, Artigas refused to abide by it because it meant that Uruguay would return to Spanish rule. He took his army on a long march away from Montevideo called the Exodus of the Orientals (those from the east bank of the river). They were joined by 16,000 people who supported his cause. In 1813 he wrote a document known as Instructions of Year 13. This outlined the principles of independence and confederation for Uruguay. He was eventually forced to leave Uruguay when the Brazilians took over in 1820. He was exiled in Paraguay where the dictator of the country held him captive until his death in 1850.

THE 19TH CENTURY (1830–1903)

This period was one of great internal political turmoil in Uruguay. The first constitution was established in 1830 with General José Fructuoso Rivera, formerly a lieutenant in Artigas' army, as president. In 1835 General Manuel Oribe succeeded Rivera as president. But in 1838, Rivera deposed Oribe and took over Montevideo. Oribe sought help from Buenos Aires and came back to lay siege to Montevideo. From 1838 to 1851 the two forces fought over Montevideo in what became known as the *Guerra Grande* or Long War.

At one battle in 1836, the two sides distinguished themselves with different colored hatbands: Oribe's forces wore white *(blanco)*, while Rivera's wore red *(colorado)*. Rivera's supporters tended to be urban-based and later formed a political party known as the Colorados, while Oribe's supporters were rural-based and formed the Blanco Party.

From the end of the Long War until 1903, the two factions continued to fight and struggle for control over Uruguay's politics. At the end of the century, after a series of conflicts and treaties, a system of sharing power between the two dominant parties was devised. This system, known as coparticipation, affected Uruguayan politics throughout the 20th century.

THE TRIPLE ALLIANCE Apart from the internal struggles, Uruguay also participated in a war against Paraguay called the War of the Triple Alliance. Francisco Solano López, then dictator of Paraguay, threatened Uruguayan independence, claiming he would take a port on the Río de la Plata for his country. In 1865 the "Triple Alliance" of Brazil, Argentina, and Uruguay went to war against Paraguay. The Paraguayans were outnumbered 10 to one and after six years of fighting, the Paraguayan population was virtually decimated. The war ended in 1870 with Paraguay in total defeat.

Between 1870 and 1903 there were 25 different presidents. Of these, nine were forced out of power, two were assassinated, one suffered a grave injury, 10 had to resist one or more attempted revolutions, and only three were problem-free.

MODERN URUGUAY

BATLLE AND BATLLISMO (1903–66) José Batlle ("bahj-jay") y Ordóñez served as president during two periods, 1903–07 and 1911–15. During these eight years he initiated far-reaching reforms that determined the future of Uruguay for more than 60 years. This legacy of political, social, and economic reform is known as Batllismo ("bahj-JEES-moh").

He believed the Uruguayan economy was too small to be left in the hands of private interests, especially when they were foreign. So he began "autonomous entities," which were government-owned industries with a monopoly over certain types of manufacturing or export goods. Since they were under the control of the government, these industries could be taxed according to need and the rights of workers would be protected.

Batlle also believed that politics and religion should be separated so that divorce became purely a civil matter. Among his more important reforms are the following: abolition of income tax for low-paid public employees (1905); establishment of secondary schools in every major city

Batlle was born into a strong Colorado family, and his father, Lorenzo Batlle y Grau, served as president from 1868 to 1872. Batlle himself founded a Colorado Party newspaper, El Día, *in 1886 and wrote about politics throughout his life.*

THE MASSACRE AT SALSIPUEDES

Ironically, *sal-si-puedes* ("SAHL-see-poo-AY-days") means "leave if you can" and is the name of the place where the last large group of Charrúa Indians were killed and captured by European Uruguayans. After independence from Brazil in 1828, the new government decided that the Indians who had fought so bravely with Artigas had to be destroyed. The excuse they used was that the Charrúa were stealing settlers' cattle. The president at the time, General Fructuoso Rivera, was trusted by the Charrúa. In 1831 he sent them a message that they were needed by the army to defend the borders against the Brazilians at Salsipuedes. When the Indians arrived—some 340 men, women, and children—they set up camp, exchanged gifts with the army officers, and turned in for the night. The army of 1,200 soldiers attacked the group, killing 40 Charrúa fighters and capturing the remaining 300. These Charrúa were forced to march to Montevideo where they were enslaved as household servants. By 1840 there were only 18 surviving Charrúa in Uruguay.

(1906); the right for women to sue for divorce on grounds of cruelty (1907); establishment of state banks (1912); creation of an autonomous agency to run the port of Montevideo (1912); nationalization of the telephone utility (1915); provision of credit to the rural poor through state banks; and drafting a new constitution. The constitution was passed after his second term in 1919.

Perhaps Batlle's most enduring legacy was a system of government he created called the *colegiado* ("koh-lay-hee-AH-doh") or collegiate system. Between 1907 and 1911 he traveled extensively in Europe, and was most impressed with the Swiss system of government in which there is no single president but rather a panel of people in control of the executive. He supported the creation of a new constitution that divided the powers of government between the president and a nine-member collegiate with six representatives from the party that won the elections and three from the losing party. In a sense, this was a continuation of the 19th century struggle for coparticipation between the two big political parties. The new constitution also guaranteed the secret ballot and a system of voting called "double simultaneous balloting." Most other politicians of the time rejected the collegiate idea, but when Batlle threatened to run for the presidency a third time if they did not pass the constitution, they agreed to the idea.

Democracy, loosely defined, was maintained throughout this period, but competition for control of the collegiate and efforts to abolish it by both parties continued. During the Great Depression (1930s), there was a brief suspension of elections as two factions, one from each party, tried to control the government. However, with the improvement in exports resulting from the Korean War (1950–53), democracy was re-established. Uruguay had one of the most stable regimes in Latin America throughout the first half of the 20th century. All that would change in the 1960s.

Batlle promoted social welfare for the poor and the working class, education for all, national control of important sectors of the economy, and a secular or non-religious state. The heritage of Batllismo made Uruguay what it is today, for better and for worse. Everything from the class system to current economic problems to the state of health and welfare are the result of Batlle's vision. Whether Uruguayans agreed with him or not, they recognize that he was a brilliant and powerful man who wanted the best for his people.

25

REPRESSION AND DICTATORSHIP (1966–84) Although Batllismo created a relatively stable government with an educated population protected by a large social welfare system, it also left a legacy of too much government spending. When the export economy was booming, this worked fine, but when there were slowdowns in the demand for Uruguay's main exports (beef, hides, wool), the government was left with huge expenditures and little income. This meant heavy borrowing, which resulted in inflation. The cost of living for Uruguayans doubled between 1959 and 1962, and again between 1962 and 1964. Inflation rose to 100% by 1965. People wanted change, starting with the collegiate system.

The Colorados were elected in 1966 under Oscar Gestido, who abolished the collegiate and gave more powers to the president. When he died in 1968, his vice-president, Areco Pacheco, took power and began to

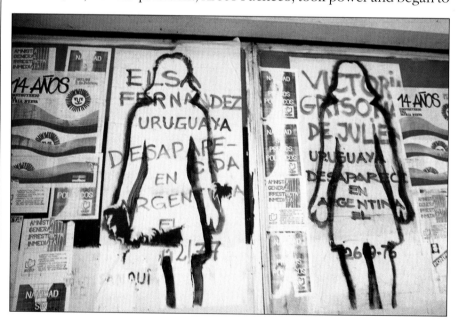

Wall drawings demanding the return of the "disappeared" people in Salto in 1985.

26

outlaw various left-wing groups, newspapers, and small political parties that had sprung up in response to the economic crisis.

Repression and suspension of civil rights continued and intensified in the late 1960s in response to a newly formed revolutionary group called the Tupamaros. The group began an armed struggle against a government that they believed was selling Uruguay to foreign interests at the cost of the well-being of Uruguayans. They were responsible for many acts of terrorism, but the two most notable were the kidnapping of Daniel Mitrione, an American, in 1970, and Jeoffrey Jackson, the British ambassador, in 1971.

While most Uruguayans did not want violence, there was a growing sense that a new political party was needed to represent the people. In the 1971 election, a new group called the Frente Amplio (Broad Front) ran for power. This was a coalition of left-wing political groups headed by Wilson Ferreira. To the shock and dismay of the other two more conservative parties, the Frente Amplio took 30% of the vote in Montevideo and 18% of the national vote. Juan María Bordaberry of the Colorados was sworn in as president, but many suspected fraud.

During the whole period of government repression, the military had been growing in strength and power and was increasing its pressure on the president to do things its way. For the first two years of Bordaberry's presidency, the military stayed in the wings trying to control him indirectly, but in 1973, it lost its patience and, in a coup, deposed Bordaberry and established a dictatorship. The main causes for the military takeover were economic decline, social unrest among workers and students, terrorism by the Tupamaros, and ineffective politicians. By 1973 the military had effectively wiped out the Tupamaros, but it continued to use them as an excuse to justify the abuse of civil rights.

Between 1968 and 1971, military expenditure grew from 13.9% to 26.2% of the national budget, while education expenditure fell from 24.3% to 16.6% in the same period. For a country that had always prided itself on a superb education system, this was an alarming trend.

Opposite: The military is a noticeable presence in Uruguay. Governments trying to restructure the economy are caught between the military and the workers, leaving them little room to maneuver.

THE TUPAMAROS

This group was founded in 1963 under the leadership of a socialist law student, Raul Sendic. He became involved with the plight of poor agricultural workers and vowed to help them against a government that refused to increase their wages despite high inflation. Aside from some small marches and thefts of food, the Tupamaros did not emerge as a real threat until the mid-1960s when they began to rob banks to fund their activities. They followed a policy of not harming innocent people during their raids and gained much popular support. They wanted the government to stop repressing workers and stop taking loans and direction from foreign powers, specifically the United States. Many Uruguayans felt that change was needed and violence seemed the only way to make it happen.

Tupamaro ("too-pah-MAH-roh") is a short version of *Tupac Amaru,* the name of an Incan chief who led a rebellion against the Spanish colonial government in Peru in 1780. He was caught and drawn and quartered, and has been a symbol of resistance for South Americans since that time.

During the dictatorship, the number of military and police personnel nearly doubled to an all-time high of 64,000 in 1978, and they were used to keep Uruguayans in a state of constant fear. As a result, 10% of Uruguayans left the country, never to return. The education system was virtually dismantled; 80% of university professors and 40–50% of public school teachers were arrested, fired, or left their jobs in fear of torture.

One of the main goals of the military government was to improve Uruguay's economy. Unfortunately, they came into power just as the worldwide oil crisis started in 1973, when the oil-producing nations decided to raise the price of gas and oil. Every country dependent on imported oil suffered during this time and tried to generate more money by protecting its own industry through trade tariffs. The Uruguayan military thought they could stimulate the economy by opening it to foreign investment. This only made things worse as small Uruguayan companies could not compete and went under. Government spending on social programs was cut and wages were frozen, which increased poverty. Continued loss of income from falling exports resulted in heavy borrowing from international banks; by 1981 Uruguay's debt was US$4 billion. With a population of only three million, this was a staggering amount.

RETURN TO DEMOCRACY (1984–PRESENT)

The end of military rule began in 1980 with the failure of a plebiscite organized by the military that would have guaranteed them continued power. Elections were promised for 1984, though the military still insisted that certain left-wing parties could not participate. However, faced with worsening economic conditions, the military reluctantly gave power and responsibility back to civilian rulers. Eventually, the three main parties and the military agreed on a new constitution, and elections were held as planned.

The challenge for subsequent democratic governments has been to revive an economy suffering from an incredible debt burden and labor unrest; rebuild the education system after years of neglect; mediate between the military and groups who want to see them tried and jailed for their crimes; and continue to support a large military budget to prevent another coup. Since 1984 politics have not been calm in Uruguay, though democracy has survived. The military has continued to be a threat to civilian rule through indirect pressures applied to the president. Sadly, this will probably continue to hamper Uruguay's attempts to rebuild well into the future.

GOVERNMENT

FOR MOST OF THE 20TH CENTURY, Uruguay has maintained a consistent democratic government system with two traditional parties. Since the military dictatorship and subsequent return to democracy, the country has faced many difficulties and new parties have emerged to challenge traditional leadership.

STRUCTURE OF GOVERNMENT

EXECUTIVE Uruguay is a republic. The president is the head of state, and he is aided by a vice-president and a 12-member council of ministers appointed by the president. Since 1966, when the collegiate system was replaced by a new constitution, the position of the president has been quite strong as he controls the appointments of the council.

Left: **The Legislative Palace in Montevideo.**

Opposite: **A policeman patrolling the streets of Montevideo.**

The military has been relatively strong since its dictatorship, but it is now subject to presidential control through the minister of defense. Military service is voluntary, and there are three branches of the service: army, navy, and air force.

The council of ministers includes the following departments: interior; foreign affairs; economy and finance; transportation and public works; health; labor and social security; livestock, agriculture, and fisheries; education and culture; defense; industry, energy, and mining; tourism; and territorial regulation and environment.

LEGISLATIVE There is a bicameral congress that provides checks and balances to the president's power: the senate consists of 30 elected representatives headed by the vice-president and the chamber of deputies consists of 99 elected representatives. There are 19 departments, each with an elected governor. Uruguay's departments are not like states since their autonomy is quite limited. Most decisions are made by the national government.

JUDICIARY There are five members in the Supreme Court, who are elected by congress and serve for 10-year terms. They can be reappointed after a break of five years. The Supreme Court appoints all other judges in the country. There are four courts of appeal, each with three judges. Civil and criminal courts are separate. Each department also has a high court and there are 224 lower courts.

THE URUGUAYAN FLAG

The flag of Uruguay was designed and approved in 1830 at the time of independence. There are four light blue stripes alternating with five white ones. These are the colors of Argentina and symbolize Uruguay's former connection with Buenos Aires during colonial times. There is also a white patch with the Sun of May in gold on it. The Sun of May has 16 rays that are alternately straight and wavy, symbolizing independence.

THE ELECTORAL PROCESS

A person can only be elected president if he or she has not served in that position for at least three months prior to the election. This serves to prevent people from taking over the position for life. Elections are held every five years, and all government positions are elected simultaneously and proportionally. Everyone over 18 years of age is eligible to vote. Voting in Uruguay is very confusing since it combines primaries and final elections. This is called the "double simultaneous ballot," which is explained below.

The Uruguayan constitution provides for direct public participation in government decisions. If people are unhappy with a decision, they can force the government to hold a national referendum. This means that the issue is put to all voters to decide. To do this, 25% of those eligible to vote must first sign a petition requesting the referendum. Once that number of signatures is gathered, the government must hold the vote within 60 days and must abide by the results.

Double Simultaneous Ballot

When an election is held, every political party can run more than one candidate for the office of president. People vote for their choice as usual, but the tricky part comes when the votes are counted. The winner is not the person with a simple majority of votes, but the person with the most votes from the party with the most votes!

Let us take an example to demonstrate how this works. To make it simple, we shall assume that only two parties, the Colorados and Blancos, are running candidates for office, and that each of them offers two candidates for president. When the votes are counted, the totals are as follows:

Colorados		Blancos	
Candidate A	25	Candidate C	10
Candidate B	30	Candidate D	35
Total	55		45

Candidate D has the simple majority of votes, but the Colorados got the most votes of the two parties, therefore one of their candidates will win—the one with the greater number of votes, Candidate B.

The double simultaneous ballot affects how political parties are run. The different factions within each political party may represent widely different ideas and platforms. In other words, people who are very conservative may vote for a candidate from one of the parties, while people who are very liberal may vote for a different candidate from the same party.

33

POLITICAL PARTIES

Uruguay has a multiparty political system with three main players in modern elections: the Blancos, generally the minority party; the Colorado Party, which has held the presidency almost continuously since independence; and the Frente Amplio, which has emerged as a coalition of fairly radical left-wing groups.

The Blanco Party, which is also known as the National Party, was formed under General Manuel Oribe in the 19th century. It tends to represent rural and conservative elements of the population. It was the Blancos that forced Batlle to include proportional representation and the secret ballot in the constitution of 1919. Although they are considered the second largest party and the traditional opponents of the Colorados, they have held the presidency only three times since Uruguay's independence from Brazil: 1835–38, 1958–67, and 1989–94.

The Colorado Party tends to represent the urban middle class, which is the largest group in Uruguay. Batlle y Ordóñez forged the party into a mature political organ, but his radical reforms also split the party into factions. Some of his party members supported his idea of a collegiate system, while others did not. Although the collegiate system has long been abandoned in Uruguay, these factions in the Colorado Party still exist.

The Frente Amplio or Broad Front, a party made up of a coalition of many smaller parties and party factions, was formed in 1971 to oppose increasing repression by the government. In the 1971 election, the Frente Amplio won 18.3% of the vote, but once the military took power, the party was outlawed. The party leaders were jailed or went into exile during the dictatorship. When democracy returned in 1984, it won 21.3% of the popular vote, demonstrating that its support was growing. The Frente Amplio is quite left-wing as it includes Communists, Socialists, Christian Democrats, and radical splinter groups from the two major parties.

The Communist Party became an official party in 1921 and has always been considered very radical. Its members were founding members of the Frente Amplio in 1971. During the dictatorship and first election, the Communist Party was outlawed. The government recognized it in 1985, and in the 1989 election, it won about 10% of the vote.

The Socialists were organized as a party in 1910, but in 1921, a majority of the members broke away to form the more radical Communist Party. Throughout the 20th century, the Socialists have become increasingly left-wing, opposing foreign investment in Uruguay for example. Some members of the Socialist Party helped form the armed guerrilla group, the Tupamaros. They are still part of the Frente Amplio coalition.

Finally, there is the Christian Democratic Party. This is the first Catholic political party in Uruguay, and was founded in 1910. It has traditionally not received more than 3–5% of the vote. It joined the Frente Amplio coalition in 1971, and again in 1984.

Generally, the Colorados are considered to be more liberal than the Blancos, but even so, it was a Colorado president, Juan María Bordaberry, that allowed the military to gain power in Uruguay in the early 1970s.

CURRENT POLITICAL SITUATION

In the presidential election held on November 27, 1994, Julio Sanguinetti of the Colorado Party was elected president and Dr. Hugo Batalla became vice-president. The Frente Amplio won the mayorship of Montevideo, indicating that the urban middle class is becoming increasingly supportive of left-wing politics.

Uruguayans are keen on keeping abreast of the latest local and international news.

Since the military dictatorship ended, elections have been held on time and with no serious problems. However, some of the economic and moral issues left by the military and by Batllismo continue to plague the government. For example, to help reduce the financial burden on the government, it has been suggested that some of the autonomous entities (government-owned industries) be privatized. These industries were part of Batlle's plan to control the Uruguayan economy, but over time they have become quite inefficient. Uruguayans are afraid that if they are privatized many people will lose their jobs, so they oppose these proposals by forcing the government to hold referendums.

The military's legacy is still felt in the education system. The military virtually destroyed the universities, and it has been very expensive for the democratic governments to try to rebuild them as useful and modern research facilities.

Uruguay is trying to expand its productivity and sales by joining other South American countries in special trade agreements. Uruguay seems to be safely democratic once again, but it faces many challenges to ensure that its people continue to be among the best-educated and healthiest in South America.

TWO-TIME PRESIDENT:
JULIO MARÍA SANGUINETTI CAIROLO

Sanguinetti was elected in 1984 in a narrow victory over the Blanco opposition. During his first presidency, his most difficult challenge was to negotiate the issue of bringing police and military personnel to justice for human rights abuses during the military dictatorship. There was public demand for public trials to make those officers responsible for death and torture face penalties. The military refused, saying its officers had just been protecting public security and could not be considered criminals for their actions. Sanguinetti managed to get an amnesty law passed, but the Frente Amplio organized a petition to demand a referendum. Fortunately for the government, the referendum failed and the amnesty was granted. Sanguinetti realized that if he were to force trials, the military would probably take over the government again.

In his second term, 1994–99, this same ability to find the best possible solution is evident. Although he could have appointed anyone to the council of ministers, Sanguinetti decided to create a government in which almost all political parties had some representation. He called this his "pact of governability" and instituted it to protect the democratic process.

Sanguinetti will go down in Uruguay's history as the president who negotiated the first five years of democracy following military dictatorship. He has managed difficult issues with remarkable tact, and his actions make it clear that whatever his specific political beliefs, his first commitment is to preserving the democratic process.

ECONOMY

URUGUAY OCCUPIES a special geographic and historical position as the buffer between Argentina and Brazil. These two countries are giants in physical size, population, and economic production compared to Uruguay. Uruguay has very few natural resources. It does not have large forests or mines and much of its land is unsuited to growing crops. For that reason, the original settlers turned to livestock production, which is a very significant part of the economy even today. Uruguay's population is too small to support a big industrial sector. All these factors have made it difficult for Uruguay to sustain economic growth.

In addition, Uruguay generally imports more in goods such as cars and machinery from Brazil and Argentina than it exports in food to them. This results in a trade deficit because the country is losing money by having to spend more on imports than it earns from exports.

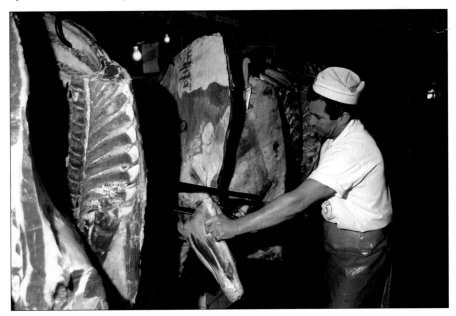

Left: **Cutting and trimming sides of beef in a processing plant in Montevideo.**

Opposite: **A bulk carrier unloading cargo on the docks of Montevideo.**

39

Uruguay's history of democracy and social welfare has also added to modern economic problems. Since Batlle's reforms at the beginning of this century (except for the period of military dictatorship), the government has tried to provide its people with good education at a reasonable cost and other welfare benefits, such as social security for retired people and wage protection. But because Uruguay's population is aging, there are too many people collecting social security and too few working and paying taxes to support them. The government has tried to raise the extra money from other sources.

Another problem is what to do with the government-owned factories and the factory workers. Although these factories provide the workers with safe and well-paid jobs, they are expensive to maintain and unprofitable.

Finally, Uruguay is experiencing a serious debt crisis. The combination of all of these factors presents Uruguay with many economic problems as it enters the next millenium.

Above: **The *peso Uruguayo* or Uruguayan peso has no international symbol, but "$U" is used within the country.**

Opposite: **Loading live sheep onto a ship for export.**

CURRENCY

The currency in Uruguay is called the *peso Uruguayo* or Uruguayan peso ("PAY-soh"). It is divided into 100 cents. Because of inflation and soaring prices in 1993, the old currency was changed, so that 1,000 of the old pesos became one new peso. With the new currency, prices now look affordable again and the currency is stronger on the international market. One US dollar was worth 10.315 Uruguayan pesos at May 1998 rates of exchange.

MAIN INDUSTRIES

AGRICULTURE Agricultural products are the primary source of exports. About 41 million acres (16.6 million hectares) of land are devoted to agriculture, and approximately 90% of this land is used to raise animals that produce meat and dairy products, wool, hides, and leather goods. Uruguay has over 25 million sheep, 10 million head of cattle, 500,000 horses, and about 223,000 pigs. On 10% of its arable land, Uruguay produces rice, sugarcane, wheat, barley, potatoes, and sorghum. Six million fruit trees produce peaches, oranges, tangerines, and pears.

There are three agricultural zones in the country: the southern zone, which produces fruit and vegetables for people living in Montevideo; the northern zone where the sheep and cattle ranches are; and the eastern zone where grains and cereals are grown.

About 50% of all exports come directly from agricultural production (fruit and raw meat, for example) or indirectly from manufacturing of agricultural goods (for example, canned meat). Agriculture produces about 11% of the total money made in any given year. The remainder of economic activity is in mining of semiprecious stones like amethyst and topaz, fishing, hydroelectric power production, and forestry.

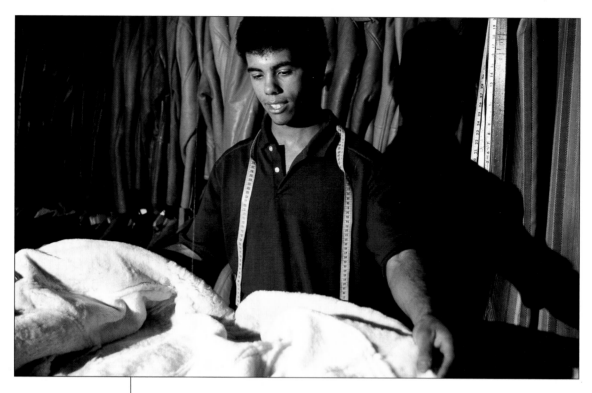

A young salesman and cutter in a leather factory preparing the hides for manufacture into jackets.

MANUFACTURING Although agriculture accounts for most exports, manufacturing and construction contribute 25% of the country's total income in a given year. The main manufacturing industries are meat packing, oil refining, cement manufacture, food and beverage processing, leather and cloth manufacturing, and chemical processing. Still, manufacturing depends on farming, since many of the factories produce food or clothing made from wool and leather.

SERVICE SECTOR The biggest share of the national economy is produced by the service sector. This includes businesses like restaurants, hotels, transportation, communications, community services, and any other service that people pay for in daily life. One of the services Uruguay offers to the world is its special banking system. Banks in Uruguay, like those in Switzerland, keep all accounts completely private; no one else can find out who has money in them or how much they have. The service sector accounts for about 38% of the country's total income every year.

INTERNATIONAL TRADE

Uruguay's primary trade partners are Brazil, Argentina, the United States, and Germany. The biggest export commodities are live animals and animal products such as milk, meat, fish, vegetables, rice, processed food and drinks, wool, woollen cloth and clothing, and hides and leather products. The main imports from these countries include machinery and household appliances, transportation equipment like cars and airplanes, metals and metal products, petroleum products like oil and gas, and chemicals. This reflects Uruguay's position as primarily an agricultural country with few natural resources of its own.

In 1995 a new trade agreement between Uruguay, Paraguay, Brazil, and Argentina came into effect. MERCOSUR, short for Mercado del Sur or Southern Market, is a free-trade agreement where participating countries

Uruguay has insufficient mineral and energy resources. For this reason, oil products are totally imported and then refined in refineries such as this one near Montevideo.

trade with one another without charging any taxes on imports and exports. For a small country like Uruguay, MERCOSUR means that no added taxes are levied on food and clothing exports to the large populations of Brazil and Argentina. If Uruguay can make a pound of meat more cheaply than Brazil, then its meat will sell more cheaply in Brazilian supermarkets. This is a great advantage for all the countries involved. Chile is trying to join MERCOSUR. This would make the total population of producers and consumers even bigger.

There are plans to build a bridge across the Río de la Plata connecting Colonia and Buenos Aires. When this is completed, Uruguay will be able to export more of its fruit and vegetables to the big markets in Buenos Aires. Right now, it is quite expensive to ship this food over the river or to drive the long way around through Paysandú.

THE DEBT CRISIS

Since the 1980s, one of the biggest and most persistent problems faced by all countries in South America is their foreign debt. Just like individuals who go to banks to borrow money in order to buy a house or a car, countries go to special international banks, like the World Bank, to borrow money. When you borrow money from a bank, you have to agree to pay back the money in a certain time with interest. Uruguay, like many of its neighbors, faces a debt crisis because it owes far more money than it can make. Just to give you some idea of how serious this is, in 1985, Uruguay, with a population of only 3 million people, owed US$4.9 billion dollars. If the debt were shared, each Uruguayan man, woman, and child would owe about US$1,600 to foreign banks. Since the minimum wage is only about US$90 per month, this is a huge debt burden. When it looks as if a country cannot afford to pay back its loans, the International Monetary Fund (IMF) steps in. It tells the country what to do in order to make more money to pay its debt. This usually involves cutbacks in spending, limits on wages and prices, and cutbacks in social services. The government of Uruguay tried to do this in 1990, but people protested. This whole situation is responsible for much of the labor problems in Uruguay and in all of Latin America today.

ENERGY, TRANSPORTATION, COMMUNICATIONS

Uruguay provides its own hydroelectric power from dams on its many rivers. One of the largest is at Salto Grande on the Río Uruguay. Uruguay imports petroleum products from Argentina. Crude oil is also imported and then refined into usable forms in Uruguay.

Uruguay has one of the best highway systems in all of South America. Of the 31,000 miles (50,000 km) of roads, about 80% are rural dirt roads; the rest are paved or graveled. The railway system is owned by the government and is used primarily for transporting goods rather than people. The principal shipping ports are Montevideo, Punta del Este, Colonia, Fray Bentos, Paysandú, and Salto. There are two international airports: Montevideo and Punta del Este. For travel within the country, there are 14 other airports with permanent runways.

Most telecommunications facilities are centered in Montevideo where the majority of the people live. With over 350,000 telephones in operation, Uruguay has the highest number of telephones per capita in South America.

LABOR FORCE

There are just over one million workers in Uruguay. They are considered to be the best-educated workforce in Latin America. Retirement age is 55 for women and 60 for men, and the minimum wage is about US$90 per month. According to 1994 figures, this is the distribution of workers in the various sectors: 40% in the service sector, 22% in manufacturing, 17% in trade, 8% in agriculture, 7% in construction, and 6% in transportation and communications. Unemployment in 1996 was about 12%.

Workers have been organized into unions since the 19th century. The unions have been quite effective in guaranteeing good conditions and wages for their members. In the mid-20th century, many unions were associated with the Communist Party but by the 1960s, fewer than 3% of union members were affiliated with the party. Increasing repression in the late 1960s included the suppression of labor activities and the harassment of labor leaders. The military simply banned unions and strikes during the dictatorship. The return to democracy in 1984 meant a return of the unions.

There has been much labor unrest in the past two decades when the two biggest federations of unions, the PIT and CNT, organized strikes to protest inflation and falling real wages. Most of the strikes involved urban workers. In general, the majority of workers are concentrated in urban areas and organized into unions.

Rural workers, on the other hand, make up a small percentage of the total labor force and are forced to live in shantytowns and work for low wages on big farms. They face problems caused by uneven land distribution; the top 6% of landowners own 57% of the land. Uruguay is struggling to balance the needs and rights of these people with the demands of economic reform.

With inflation, prices go up quickly while wages do not. Hence a person's "real" wage falls because it does not buy as much food or clothing as it did before.

URUGUAYANS

THE DEMOGRAPHICS OF URUGUAY show some interesting and distinctive features. Demography is the study of the features of human populations including ethnic composition, age breakdown, average birth rate, and so on. Because of its unusual history, Uruguayan demographics are not typical for Latin America. This chapter looks at what the population of Uruguay is like and why it is like that.

ETHNIC GROUPS

Uruguay has one of the most homogeneous populations in South America. The majority—88% of the population—are descendants of European settlers. There are two main groups: those whose forefathers were from Spain and those whose ancestors originally came from Italy. Both groups now speak Spanish and intermingle.

The next largest ethnic group is the *mestizos* ("may-STEE-sohs"), the descendants of marriages between Indians and Spaniards during colonial times. Mestizos are 8% of the population and generally live in rural areas.

Finally, 4% of the population is of African descent. Most of this group are descended from slaves brought from Africa in the 18th and early 19th centuries. They live mostly in Montevideo where the largest concentration of slaves were. Some members of this African-Uruguayan group live along the northern border with Brazil. They came to Uruguay from Brazil.

Though Uruguay is an open and tolerant society, racism still persists among different ethnic groups.

Above: **Mestizos, like this boy, make up 8% of Uruguay's total population.**

Opposite: **A young girl of European descent.**

49

Above: **African-Uruguay-ans, like this couple, make up 4% of the population.**

Opposite: **A middle-aged couple of Italian descent, from the department of Maldonado.**

IMMIGRATION, MIGRATION, EMIGRATION

As with many New World nations, the bulk of the modern population are descended from immigrants from all over the world. First were the Spaniards, who started settling in Uruguay in the 18th century. The next group to arrive were African slaves, who were used mostly as domestic servants. After abolition, they stayed on to form a small but vital subculture in the country.

European migration to Uruguay has changed through the years. Originally, under colonialism, only Spaniards were encouraged to move to the New World. After independence, however, the new government realized that more people were needed to settle the interior and develop the country. From 1830 to 1870, there was a boom in European migration, with Spanish, French, and Italians making up the immigrant groups. In 1860 it was estimated that 35% of the population was foreign-born. Nearer the turn of the century, Italians became the biggest group of new immigrants.

The last wave of European immigration came at the beginning of the 20th century through to the 1930s. Most of these immigrants were Jews from parts of Europe where their religion was not tolerated. Some were Spanish and Portuguese Jews, but in the 1930s, the majority were from Germany. Immigration has slowed down dramatically since the 1950s.

Once in Uruguay, most migrants chose to live in and around Montevideo and other large urban centers. Today, Uruguay is one of the most urbanized countries in the world. Eighty-eight percent of Uruguayans live in urban areas. At least 44% of the total population live in Montevideo alone, and another 12% are in the neighboring department of Canelones. The general pattern is that those born in small villages move to the capital city of their department to look for work, while those born in these department capitals tend to move to Montevideo. With so few people left in the countryside, Uruguay is almost a city-state.

Argentina was also in need of immigrants and sent agents to Italy to recruit people. But the Italians did not know much about South America and often confused Argentina and Uruguay. In 1890 the Uruguayan government actively encouraged immigration by promising able-bodied arrivals food and shelter for eight days after landing and free transportation to the interior of the country. Consequently, many people who originally planned to go to Argentina ended up in Uruguay instead.

Official figures suggest that 180,000 Uruguayans emigrated in the period 1963–75. The peak of outward migration was in 1973–75: 30,000 left in 1973, 60,000 in 1974, and nearly 40,000 in 1975. For the duration of the dictatorship, 1975–85, another 150,000 Uruguayans left the country.

As well as movement into and within the country, there has also been a steady pattern of emigration or people leaving the country. This is a far more recent trend and one that has slowed down in recent times, but it has contributed to Uruguay's modern demographic problems. The emigration of the young and educated started when the country began to experience serious economic problems in the 1960s and continued during the military dictatorship in the 1970s. Most went to Argentina where they could blend in quite well, but the United States, Australia, Spain, Brazil, and Venezuela were also popular destinations. When Sanguinetti became the first democratically elected president in 1984, he invited all exiles and migrants back. Sadly, only a few returned. Many who visited shortly after the election were so shocked by the poor state of the country that they decided never to return.

THE SLAVE TRADE

The slave trade had been in existence for some time when the Spanish crown made it legal in 1791. At that time, Montevideo was declared the official slave-trading port for the Río de la Plata area. Many ships arrived bringing Africans who had been taken forcefully from their homes and brought to the New World to be sold. Despite their social position, slaves participated in all the major wars of the 19th century, including the independence movement when they fought with Artigas. The first step to end slavery came in 1825 when trading for new slaves was prohibited and all slaves born in Uruguay were given their freedom. There were other laws aimed at ending slavery, but it was not until 1853 that all African-Uruguayans finally gained their freedom.

Aside from fighting alongside their White countrymen in all conflicts of the 19th century, African-Uruguayans also contributed to Uruguayan culture.

AN AGING POPULATION

Uruguay has an unusual demographic pattern. With the slow-down in immigration halfway through the 20th century and an acceleration in emigration, Uruguay lost and did not replace its youth. The average age of the population increased when the entry of young immigrants declined. It increased even more in the 1960s and 1970s when young people left by the thousands.

This trend was enhanced by changes in the birth and death rates in the 20th century. Advances in medicine made it possible for people to live longer, and the introduction of birth control made it possible for families to have fewer children. When both the birth rate and the death rate decrease, the average age of the population increases, as people grow up and fewer children are born. By contrast, most South American countries have the reverse problem of huge populations under the age of 15 due to high birth and low death rates. Uruguay is more like North American countries in its demographics than it is like its neighbors.

Population growth in Uruguay is one of the lowest in Latin America. This is one of the reasons why the aged make up a large portion of the population.

SOCIAL CLASSES

Uruguay is distinctive in terms of its class system too. Although there are rich people and poor people, the country has a large middle class. Roughly 5% of the population can be considered extremely wealthy, while about 50% would be considered working class, leaving 45% in the middle.

Class distinctions are not clear-cut, but generally, those at the top own lots of land or big businesses or control politics. Those in the middle own medium-sized farms or businesses, work for the government, teach, or are professionals like doctors and dentists.

The lower segment includes rural workers who own no land, farmers with small plots of land, and blue-collar workers such as those who work in factories. The unemployed in both the cities and the countryside are also included in the lower class.

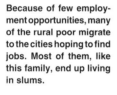

Because of few employment opportunities, many of the rural poor migrate to the cities hoping to find jobs. Most of them, like this family, end up living in slums.

GALEANO: URUGUAY'S BEST KNOWN WRITER

Eduardo Hughes Galeano was born in Montevideo in 1940. He started writing for a literary journal called *La Marcha*, which was well-known for its high quality of writing. He left the country during the repression to live in Spain. He returned in 1984 to become the editor of a new journal, *Brecha*. The military had shut down *La Marcha*.

His most famous book is *Open Veins of Latin America*, a history of Latin America from the European conquest to 1971 (when the book was first published). It is a political commentary on how the people of Latin America have been used first by the Spanish and Portuguese and then by other more powerful nations. This book has been published in over 30 editions and is still on reading lists in universities around the world. More recently, he has written an interesting trilogy, *Memory of Fire*, published in 1988. This is a collection of stories, poems, newspaper articles, and reports detailing life in Latin America from before the European conquest to the present. It complements *Open Veins*, which is more of a straightforward history.

Galeano has also written fiction. His most notable novel, *Days and Nights of Love and War*, is about living with a military dictatorship. This is based on experiences in Uruguay.

LIFESTYLE

THIS CHAPTER looks at what life is like for Uruguayans. It begins with a description of the national character and dress, and moves on to lifestyles in the cities and countryside and family life. Descriptions of women's lives and rights, and of gauchos, a special group from the past, are included in this chapter.

NATIONAL CHARACTER AND DRESS

Most Uruguayans describe themselves as cultured, generous, conservative, and serious but quite often sad. They do not like to be ridiculed and tend to be cautious—they try never to rush into things. They are humble about themselves and very family-oriented.

On the negative side, they say they are frequently late. In fact, one joker has said, "In Uruguay, nothing starts on time because if one is punctual, one is alone."

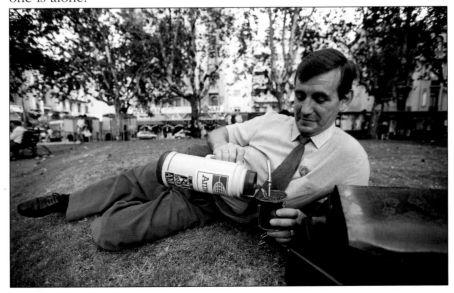

Left: **For this man, a break from the office means relaxing in the park and sipping the Uruguayan's favorite drink, *mate*.**

Opposite: **A view of the Punta del Este skyline from Cantegril Beach.**

57

Uruguayans consider themselves quite family-oriented. Aunts, uncles, cousins, and grandparents are always part of daily family life.

Uruguayans are also fiercely egalitarian—they prefer to make things equal for everyone. As this has been part of the general government design, it is no surprise that people's character reflects this.

The two passions that unite Uruguayans are soccer and *mate*, a herbal tea. It is said that "Uruguayan males are born with a diploma in soccer under their arms." This is definitely their national sport. *Mate* for them is something like coffee for many North Americans. People drink it throughout the day, and Uruguayans can often be seen carrying a thermos of hot water to use for making *mate*.

One feature of Uruguayan character that stems from the indigenous past is something called the *Garra Charrúa* ("GAR-rah char-ROO-ah") or Charrúan Talon. *Garra Charrúa* refers to character traits of persistence, fierceness, and bravery. When Uruguayans have to do something difficult or dangerous, they say they have the *Garra Charrúa* qualities of courage and fierceness.

There is no national dress or manner of dressing that distinguishes Uruguayans from any other people of European descent. About the only thing that distinguishes urban Latin Americans from urban Americans is that dress codes are often slightly more formal in the south. Latin American women also tend to dress more often in skirts than in pants.

The only traditional dress one finds in Uruguay comes from the gauchos. The gaucho or cowboy heritage of Uruguay is very important and people work hard at preserving it.

RURAL AND URBAN CLASSES

THE RURAL CLASSES Historically, the interior of the country was settled slowly as people moved to the open grasslands to be closer to their cattle, sheep, and horses. Gradually, during the 19th century, fences were built to create large ranches, called *estancias* ("ay-STAN-see-ahs"). The soil in the grasslands is not rich enough for intensive farming, so these *estancias* are used to pasture herds of animals. To run a ranch, only a few people are needed to make sure the fences are mended and the animals are well. There are a couple of class divisions among rural people and this makes for a difference in lifestyle.

Ranch owners typically do not live on their isolated ranches. Those who own big plots of land (65,000 acres/26,325 hectares is not uncommon) are quite wealthy and prefer to live in Montevideo where their families have access to the best private schools and all other urban services. Even the big agricultural fair is held in Montevideo every year. These ranching elites have traditionally supported the Blanco Party and in general are more conservative than the urban-based elites. So if they live in the city, who is running the ranch?

The large *estancias* are usually divided into areas for different uses—one for cattle, one for sheep, and one for crops (usually animal feed). Each area is managed by a foreman. The foremen are often related to the ranch owners. Under the foreman is the ranger, who is like a modern gaucho. The rangers, in turn, may manage a few ranch hands or helpers, who do some of the more menial tasks for them.

Far from the center, life in the countryside is much slower but also much more hierarchical. Ranch owners or foremen would be unlikely to socialize with their rangers or ranch hands, for example, and they would rarely permit a marriage across these divisions. Being more isolated from

There are few people on estancias *as the animals do not need much attention except in the spring when the young are born and when the ranch owner wants to sell some of the animals for meat or leather. Sheep, of course, have to be sheared to collect the wool once a year.*

Young women selling jewelry in a street flea market in Montevideo.

trends in the cities has also meant that rural workers tend to be more religious and are less likely to be members of labor unions.

Only those individuals who can afford to send their children to live in town can guarantee that they will get a high school education. The poorest 5% of the population are the ranch hands who make little money, and owners of small farms who usually cannot afford to travel to the city to take advantage of urban services.

THE URBAN CLASSES There are also class divisions in the cities. At the top of the heap are the business and political elites. These are the families that have historically controlled trade and government. The business and industrial elites during the 19th century were considered inferior to the landowning class. This changed during the 20th century so now the big ranching and business families tend to intermarry and combine their interests. Together, they form the top 5% of the population in terms of wealth.

The political elite is composed of a small group of families that have traditionally sent their sons to law school to give them a strong base from which to enter politics. Nowadays, there are more political parties, and control of the government is not restricted to a few important families. There still are "political families," but the newer parties are being led by middle-class teachers, lawyers, and civil servants.

Next down the line is the urban middle class. This group includes professionals, teachers, business managers, and those who own small businesses. They are not quite the majority of the population, but this group is definitely the one to set the standard in Uruguayan society.

GAUCHOS: THE COWBOYS OF THE SOUTH

Gaucho traditions and clothes date back to Spanish colonial times when there were no fences to mark property and cattle and sheep roamed freely. The first Spaniards to take advantage of these herds were a hardy group of expert horsemen who would ride across the plains, rounding up cattle and sheep as they went. They lived on the land and camped out for days, far from the nearest house. Their main diet was beef cooked over open fires and washed down with *mate*. These men were independent and tough.

Typical gaucho dress resulted from the demands of rough outdoor living and long days of horseback riding. Gauchos always had a large blanket with a hole in the middle that could double as a raincoat/poncho or sleeping bag. They also wore something called a *chiripá* ("chee-ree-PAH"), which was a sort of skirt worn over the seat of the trousers to protect them from wear on the saddle. The gauchos' shirts and pants were always loose and baggy to permit free movement. They wore *rastras* ("RAHS-trahs"), or wide belts made of metal, and soft leather boots. The boots had to be soft so that they could easily stand in the saddle to get a good view of the horizon. The whole outfit was topped with a soft, brimmed hat of black felt.

Essential equipment for the gaucho included a horse and saddle, a long knife called a *façon* ("FAH-sone"), and the *boleadoras* (weapon of rocks and leather thongs used to bring down big animals).

In the 1870s, wealthy people started buying pieces of land and fencing in the animals. This was the end of the gaucho era, since these fiercely independent men were forced to work for landowners—and work, moreover, in much more restricted areas. Today, there are still ranch hands on horseback, but their clothes have been modernized and their way of life is no longer carefree and independent.

The gaucho still symbolizes a glorious past of freedom and independence for modern Uruguayans. Gaucho traditions are celebrated during a special festival once a year.

A typical work day for the urban working class in Montevideo starts with the rush to get to work early in the morning.

As the economy worsened in the 1960s, middle-class women started joining the workforce to help supplement the family income. This trend mirrors what happened in North America at the same time. One critical difference is that the middle class in Uruguay can often afford to hire female servants to help around the house. This has made it easier for Uruguayan women to work without having to work at home too.

At the bottom of the income scale are the blue-collar workers and urban poor. Uruguay has never had a very large industrial workforce simply because its small size meant that there were never many industries. However, those that do work in industry have tended to maintain a reasonable standard of living with the help of the unions. All urban industries are unionized in Uruguay, and this has meant that workers have been well-protected. Like middle-class women, working-class women have had to join the workforce if they can, but since they cannot afford domestic help, they often work twice as hard. Some working-class families have been unable to earn sufficient income in the usual way to survive. Over the last few years, there has been an increase in what is known as informal sector activities. These are income-generating activities that are not reported to the government, either because people do not want to pay tax or because they are illegal. Some examples of work in the informal sector are domestic work, trading in smuggled goods from Brazil, and piecework such as sewing or knitting at home.

Also included in the lowest income group are the unemployed and retired people who live only on government pensions.

FAMILY LIFE AND GENDER ROLES

AN URUGUAYAN FAMILY As in other Latin American countries, family ties are quite strong. The ideal family model is either the nuclear or the extended family. A nuclear family includes the father and mother and their children. An extended family includes, in addition, the adult children and their spouses and children. The extended family is more likely to be found in rural areas, though recently there are more extended families in cities. This is because young married couples find it more and more difficult to afford their own apartment or house.

In the cities, family size is quite small, the average being two children per couple. As the children grow up, they will live with their parents until they themselves are married. But it is not unusual for people in their 30s to continue to live at home because they are unmarried or cannot afford a place of their own.

An Uruguayan family enjoying a Sunday picnic in the park.

COMPADRAZGO One practice that has continued in the countryside is *compadrazgo* ("cohm-pah-DRAHZ-go") or godparenthood. When a baby is baptized, the parents choose two godparents (a man and a woman not necessarily married to each other) to help the child through various stages of life. The usual pattern is for the parents to choose godparents who are richer than they are.

The relationship between godchild and godparents is lifelong: godparents help their godchildren with schooling and finding a job, as well as help them start families of their own. In return the godchild will help the godparents whenever asked and may even vote the way the godparents vote as a show of loyalty. These kinds of ties across class and family lines create a network of relations that bind a community together.

"There are no convincing reasons to limit women's education when the State invests considerable sums of money to expand the male education."

—Jose Batlle y Ordóñez

THE STRUGGLE FOR WOMEN'S RIGHTS

At the beginning of the 20th century, Uruguayan women had very few rights. Their husbands were legally responsible for them and their property. If a woman was given money or land by her father, she lost control of it when she married. She also did not have the right to sue for divorce, although a man might beat and even kill his wife if he caught her with another man. She could not vote and was basically treated as a child by the legal system. Women did not earn the same amount of money for work of comparable value and were expected to stay home and raise children.

Batlle's reforms made some progress with divorce laws, but women themselves had to organize and fight for their rights. One woman who made a difference was Paulina Luisi. She was born in 1875 and became the first Uruguayan woman to get a medical degree. Throughout her life, she was committed to children's welfare and women's rights to education and to the vote. She represented Uruguay at a number of international conferences on women's and children's issues and was the first woman to serve as an official representative of her government at an intergovernmental conference in 1923. Along with other feminists (both male and female), Luisi managed to see women get the vote in 1938 for the first time. Finally, in 1946, the Law of Civil Rights of Women was passed, guaranteeing women equality with men. Luisi died in 1950 but will always be remembered as an inspiration to all women fighting for their rights.

WOMEN'S ROLES Women in Uruguay have had the benefit of legal protection and rights for much longer than their neighbors. However, there is still an expectation that men will be "macho"—that they will be the breadwinners and heads of their families. It is quite acceptable for women to work outside the home, but they are still responsible for domestic tasks as well.

Young girls, especially in the cities, are given the same educational opportunities as boys. In the countryside, poorer families often cannot afford to send all their children to high school and will choose to educate boys over girls, believing that their future chances for getting work will be greater. Girls from these poorer families often migrate to towns or big cities to find work as domestic servants.

Boys and girls are given equal opportunities in getting an education, but poorer families will still choose to send their sons for furthur education rather than their daughters.

EDUCATION

Uruguay was the first country in Latin America to have free, universal, and compulsory education. In 1877 the Law of Common Education was passed, making education available to all school-age children. Uruguay also has one of the best education systems and literacy rates in Latin America. Literacy is estimated at 96%, and there is no difference between men and women in this regard. Also, nearly 100% of school-age children attend elementary school. The first nine years of school are compulsory; children are required to stay in school until they are 14 years old.

Schoolchildren do not have to wear uniforms, but they do have to wear smocks over their clothes. The reason for this is that it makes all children equal whether rich or poor. Public schools are free and secular. There are private schools in the cities that cater to wealthy families.

There are two universities in Uruguay, both in Montevideo. The University of the Republic is publicly supported and free to anyone who has completed high school, although students do have to pay for books and there are some small fees for the use of university facilities. The Catholic University is private and charges tuition.

The average university program takes four to six years, but most students take longer to finish. There are discounts on public transit and subsidized canteens for students; an undergraduate can ride the bus more cheaply and go to special cafeterias with cheap food. With a limited number of jobs for graduates, there is little incentive to graduate quickly. About 70% of all university students come from Montevideo.

Two classes of Uruguayans rarely go to university: the poor who start work young to help supplement the family income and rural people who cannot afford the living expenses away from home.

HEALTH

Health care, along with other social programs, is subsidized by the government. Subsidized care is not universal; those who can afford private health care are expected to pay for it. There are more than 60 public clinics and seven public hospitals in Montevideo. In the countryside, about half the departments have a hospital in their capital city; the rest have auxiliary clinics only. There are 466 people per doctor in Uruguay, a very good ratio and one comparable with developed countries. However, outside Montevideo the number is 1,234 people per doctor; inside, it is only 262. About 400,000 people have no health coverage.

The average life expectancy in Uruguay is 70 years for men and 76 years for women; infant mortality is about 22 deaths per 1,000 births. These numbers are not quite as good as in developed countries, but they are respectable by Latin American standards.

Right: **Uruguay, through its government subsidized social programs, tries to provide help for its poor.**

Opposite: **A typical apartment block where Montevideo's middle-income families live.**

HOUSING

In the cities, there are areas with apartment blocks and areas of suburban family homes. In the bigger centers, there is also public housing, which is subsidized by the government for people on low-income budgets.

In the countryside, being rich or poor makes a huge difference in how one lives. The poorest agricultural workers live in shantytowns of poorly constructed huts that do not have running water or sewage systems. By contrast, the rich live in large ranch houses. These were often built in the 19th century and have been modernized over time. They are usually big, sprawling, one-story houses. The walls are solidly constructed and the rooms are big enough to entertain many guests. Today, some of these homes are open to tourists who want to see what life is like out in the open grasslands.

Ranches are separated by great distances, so when ranch owners visited one another, they would often stay for a while. For this reason, houses had extra bedrooms and big dining rooms.

RELIGION

ALTHOUGH A HIGH PERCENTAGE OF URUGUAYANS belong to the Roman Catholic Church, the society is considered quite secular. This means that much of daily life is not at all religious. According to the constitution, no religion is recognized as official or preferred. As a result, Christmas is officially called Family Day and Easter Week is known as Tourism Week or *Semana Criolla*. Most Uruguayans are not very religious and have always tolerated other faiths. Uruguay is quite exceptional in this regard in South America, where most people are Catholic.

A SECULAR SOCIETY

Compared to most of its neighbors in South America, Uruguay has been much less influenced by the Catholic Church from colonial times to the present. Historically, Spain sent out conquerors and priests together to take over Indian societies and convert them to Catholicism. Since Uruguay had very few Indians, and they were very difficult to control, there was less need for priests. Of course, the settlers built their own churches and continued to practice their religion, but the number of priests in Uruguay was always relatively small.

When Uruguay became independent and the first constitution was written, Catholicism was the official religion, but the constitution protected the people's right to religious freedom. As early as 1844, British traders living in Montevideo were allowed to build an Anglican church for themselves. This was one of the first Protestant churches built in Spanish America. In 1935, when this church was in the way of a new sea wall planned for the city, the government paid to have it moved stone by stone to another location, because it was considered a historical landmark.

Above: **Nuns outside a church in the department of La Paz. There are approximately 1,580 Catholic sisters in Uruguay.**

Opposite: **The Cathedral of Salto. In a 1981 study, it was found that there were 221 parishes with 204 diocesan priests in Uruguay.**

A couple being photographed after their civil wedding ceremony at the registry office in Montevideo.

Since independence, Uruguay has become more and more secularized and fewer events depend on church participation. For example, in 1837 civil marriages were made legal. In 1861 the state took over public cemeteries so that the Catholic Church could not prevent non-Catholics from being buried in them. During Batlle's two terms as president (1903–07 and 1911–15), many more secular laws were passed. He believed all religions should be equally tolerated and that none should control people's lives in a legal way. In 1907 Batlle made divorce legal. In Catholicism, divorce is prohibited, and if two people want to end their marriage, they must get special permission from the church. Many Catholics believe it is a sin to divorce. With the divorce law, the state gave permission to people who wanted to end their marriage.

In 1909 all religious classes were banned from public schools. Finally, the constitution created by Batlle and passed in 1919 officially separated church and state, and Catholicism was no longer the recognized religion of Uruguay.

There are many conflicting statistics about how many people call themselves Catholic and how many people actually follow all the rules of the Church. Low estimates say that only two-thirds or about 66% of Uruguayans call themselves Catholic, while high estimates suggest 78% are Catholic. Nevertheless, at a conference of Catholic bishops in 1978, the Church reported that only about 4% of the population regularly attended church. Generally, church attendance is higher in rural areas than in the cities, and is higher among women than among men.

SOCIETY OF JESUS: THE JESUITS IN URUGUAY

The Society of Jesus was founded in 1540 in Europe. A Catholic, Ignatius Loyola, was alarmed by the Reformation, a period in the early 1500s when some Christians split away from the Roman Catholic Church and founded Protestant groups. He decided to start a new religious order to encourage more men to stay with the Catholic Church. Priests of this order call themselves Jesuits, and one of their primary goals is to convert non-Christian peoples to Catholicism. They are strictly trained in arts and sciences so that they are teachers as well as religious leaders.

Jesuits were very important in the initial stages of settlement in South America. They were among the few people brave enough to try to communicate with often hostile Indians. They also attempted to learn native languages and teach Indians how to speak Spanish. In Uruguay, Paraguay, and Argentina, the Jesuits built missions where the Indians could live and work under their protection. Sometimes these missions, called reductions, were the only safe haven from death or slavery for the native peoples.

Events in Europe in the 1700s ended the Jesuit presence in the New World. Other Catholic religious orders and some of the European royalty were very jealous of the power of Jesuits around the world. In 1767, Charles III of Spain was convinced by others to banish the Jesuits from all Spanish territory. This was a sad time for the Indians on the reductions. Many of them were taken by European settlers to be virtual slaves on their farms. Others tried to revert to their old way of life, but were not successful. An intriguing question is: would there still be a native population in Uruguay today if the Jesuits had stayed?

OTHER RELIGIONS

PROTESTANTS There have been Protestants in Uruguay at least since 1844 when the Anglican church was built. During the 20th century, many other Protestant churches were established in Uruguay. This is part of a larger trend of Protestantization in Catholic South America. Many American evangelical churches came to Uruguay and have been working hard to convert Catholics to Protestantism at least since the 1960s. Since Uruguayans are not very religious to start with, these new missionaries have only managed to form small congregations.

Some of the Protestant churches represented in Uruguay include Baptists, Adventists, Methodists, and the Evangelical Mennonite Church. They make up approximately 2% of the population.

FOLK BELIEFS

In many South American societies, folk beliefs come from indigenous cultures. The new settlers taught their religion to the natives and in exchange learned about native beliefs and superstitions. With such a small original native population, Uruguayans did not have much opportunity to learn from these original inhabitants of the country. So the folk tradition that exists in Uruguay comes from the time when many Uruguayan men were gauchos, camping and living in the open plains.

One folk belief inspired from this era is that one should not kill fireflies. These insects are thought to keep the spirits of the dead company at night with their little lights. Another rural superstition is that the seventh son will periodically turn into an animal like a wolf, pig, or goat. This is similar to the werewolf superstition that the full moon makes those who have been bitten by a wolf turn into a creature half-man and half-wolf. In Uruguay, the son born seventh in line is thought to have this curse on him and he is called *Lobizón* ("loh-bee-SON").

The symbol of the cross links all Christians but a division exists between Catholics and Protestants. Although both groups believe in Christ and the story of his life, they differ in how they choose to worship him. When the Protestants split away from the Roman Catholic Church in the early 1500s, there was tension between the two groups. Today, in most parts of the world, they coexist peacefully.

JEWS Before the repression and dictatorship, there was a sizable Jewish community in Montevideo. There were six functioning synagogues with large congregations and Jews were 2% of the total population.

Jews had migrated to Uruguay because it was known to have a religiously tolerant society. The first large wave of immigrants came at the beginning of the 20th century. The second wave of mostly German Jews came over in the 1930s when the Nazis were beginning to persecute the Jews in Germany. Many Uruguayan Jews left Uruguay during the repression in the 1970s so that now they are a small fraction of the society.

The interior of a Protestant church. From 1960 to 1985 the number of Protestants in Uruguay increased by 60% only while Protestants in the rest of Latin America increased by 500%.

LANGUAGE

AT THE SIMPLEST LEVEL, all Uruguayans are Spanish-speaking. However, the story is far more complex and interesting. This chapter considers the varieties of Spanish spoken and how Spanish has combined with other languages to create colorful dialects.

SPANISH IN THE NEW WORLD

The language spoken in Uruguay and most of the rest of South America is Spanish. That fact is taken for granted today because it is well known that the first settlers of these regions were from Spain.

However, way back when settlers were arriving from Spain, there were many languages spoken in Spain. Just to list some examples, in the 15th and 16th centuries, languages such as Catalan, Asturian, Leonese, Aragonese, Basque, and Galician were all spoken in different regions of the country. Catalan, Galician, and Basque are three that survived into the 20th century and can be heard spoken today.

Why did a particular language spoken in only some parts of Spain become the single dominant language in all of Spain's colonies in the New World? The answer is that migration to the New World followed a specific pattern.

All settlement in the New World from Spain was planned in the province of Castile in central Spain so that those wishing to apply for the right to leave Spain had to learn enough Castilian to make an application. Then they were sent to either Andalusia or Seville to wait for a boat to take them across the ocean. The waiting often took as long as a year; during that time the immigrants learned the local language.

Above and opposite: **Spanish traveled a great distance during the 15th and 16th centuries to the New World. It has become the most widely used language in Latin America including Uruguay.**

An advertisement in Spanish of a movie from the United States.

In addition, ships' crews were all from Andalusia or the Canary Islands, which had become a province of Spain in the late 1400s. Since crossing the ocean took such a long time, ships had to stop in the Canary Islands to reprovision. All New World settlers followed this route so all of them came to speak a common language by the time they arrived in their new homes. The fact that Castilian and Andalusian are quite similar reinforced this trend toward a common language. At the same time, Castilian Spanish became increasingly more common throughout Spain because it was the language of the rulers of the country. So, after five centuries, people in Latin America and in Spain both speak a language that is quite similar but not exactly the same.

The Spanish spoken in Latin America has been influenced by other factors such as time and distance. This has resulted in differences in pronunciation and word usage. Hence the Spanish of the New World settled by the Spanish is not quite the same as the language that came to dominate modern Spain.

Some of the differences in vocabulary between modern Spain and Latin America result from the time the settlers spent in port towns or onboard ships. Many words that are used every day in Latin America are only used today on boats in Spain.

Some examples are the words *botar* (to throw out), *amarrar* (to tie up), *balde* (bucket), and *timón* (steering wheel). In Spain, to throw out is *tirar*, to tie something up is *atar*, a bucket is a *cubo*, and a steering wheel is a *volante*. Other words in Latin American Spanish are from a very old form of the language and are no longer used at all in European Spanish. Some examples of these are *lindo* (beautiful), *cobija* (blanket), and *pollera* (skirt).

THE SPANISH OF URUGUAY

The official language of Uruguay is Spanish, but the reality of what people speak in daily life and why they speak that way is more complex. In Uruguay, as in any other country, there are historical influences from other languages and other times.

INFLUENCE OF THE NATIVES

Although most of the native populations were killed early in Uruguay's history, there are some remnants of their languages on the map of Uruguay. Río Yi was named by the famous Charrúas, who also used the *boleadoras*, the weapon of leather thongs and rocks used to hunt animals. This was adopted by the gauchos and is still called by its Charrúan name.

Place names like Paysandú and Yaguarí come from the language of the Guaraní. Since these populations were quite small and did not mix for very long with Spanish speakers, there are no obvious influences on Uruguayan Spanish other than these few words.

Most of the immigrants from Spain came from the Canary Islands and Galicia and they brought the peculiarities of their Spanish with them. An example is the Canary usage of *pibe/piba* for guy/gal. These words are not commonly heard outside Uruguay and Argentina.

There was also a significant number of Italian immigrants to the Río de la Plata area in the first half of the 20th century. They used their own language for a while before becoming fluent in Spanish. One of the words that has entered Uruguayan Spanish from Italian is *chau* (*ciao* in Italian), which means goodbye.

Uruguay's location between Argentina and Brazil, and the fact that it was a province of Brazil briefly in the 19th century, means that there is also a Portuguese influence in Uruguayan Spanish. There is even a whole separate language that combines Spanish and Portuguese and is spoken only along the Brazil-Uruguay border.

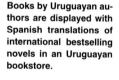

Books by Uruguayan authors are displayed with Spanish translations of international bestselling novels in an Uruguayan bookstore.

COCOLICHE AND GAUCHO SPEECH

Cocoliche was a version of Spanish spoken by Italian immigrants in the early part of the 20th century. When the first Italian immigrants were trying to learn Spanish, they found it easier to combine the two languages at first, mixing vocabulary and grammatical forms to create a very distinctive dialect. These immigrants frequently combined the language of their new country with their native tongue. The second generation grew up learning fluent Spanish in the schools and cocoliche faded away.

Gaucho speech, a rural variety of language, preserves older words and forms of grammar. To a Spanish-speaking person, gaucho speech today might be something like Shakespearean English to an American. Gaucho speech is associated with the lifestyle of these incredible men who roamed the grasslands herding wild cattle and horses. It is preserved in early poetry and novels. Today, the real gaucho is very rare and so too is their particular variety of Spanish.

Although Uruguay is not a big or populous country compared to its neighbors, it is big enough to have regional variations in language. The majority of the population lives in Montevideo where the dialect is virtually the same as that in Buenos Aires, Argentina. This dialect is called *porteño* ("por-TAYN-yoh") and is very distinctive. Part of the vocabulary of *porteño* comes from a working-class slang called *lunfardo* ("loon-FAR-doh"). The special words used by poorer people came to be used by the population as a whole through the lyrics of popular music, especially tango music.

In the interior of the country, people speak a couple of different dialects. The most notable is *fronterizo* ("fron-tayr-EE-zoh"), which is spoken close to the Brazilian border in the north. *Fronterizo* combines features of Spanish and Portuguese and is considered to be a third language. Uruguayans have learned this language because, for a long time, there have been better educational facilities and employment opportunities in Brazil than in Uruguay. The populations living along the border have therefore mixed for a long time; this combination language is the result.

Two types of speech that have passed out of use are *cocoliche* ("ko-ko-LEE-chay") and the gaucho language. These once vibrant dialects were spoken by particular groups in Uruguayan society. Because these groups no longer exist, the languages they spoke have also disappeared, but they continue to exist in poetry and the theater.

For a period in the 18th and 19th centuries, Montevideo was the main port for the trade in African slaves. Some words from African languages are still used: mucama *means a female domestic servant, and* candombe *("can-DOHM-bay") is an African-based carnival ritual and dance.*

A SIMPLE GUIDE TO SPANISH PRONUNCIATION

Spanish is one of the easiest languages to learn because what you read is what you say, as long as you know the rules of pronunciation. The Spanish alphabet has 3 extra consonants. The alphabet looks like this:

a b c ch d e f g h i j k l ll m n ñ o p q r s t u v w x y z

There are 5 main vowel sounds:

a = ah = like the a in cat, so *alma* (soul) is AHL-mah

e = ay = like the ay in day, so *mente* (mind) is MAYN-tay

i = ee = like the ee in teeth, so *infinitud* (infinity) is een-feen-ee-TOOD

o = oh = like the o in bone, so *poco* (little) is POH-koh

u = oo = like the sound in chew or zoo, so *una* (a) is OO-nah

Sometimes there are combinations of vowels, for example "ia" or "ue." Just make each vowel sound separately. So "ia" becomes ee-ah and "ue" becomes oo-ay.

Most Spanish consonants are the same as English ones, but there are a few differences:

ch = same as the English sound in church, so *che* (term of address) is chay

ll = same sound as l + y in English, so *calle* (street) is cahl-ye

ñ = same sound as n + y in English, so *mañana* (morning) is pronounced man-yan-ah

h = always silent, so *hambre* (hunger) is AM-bray

j = like the English h in hat, so *pájaro* (bird) is PAH-ha-row

qu = like the English k in keep, so *pequeño* (small) is pay-KAYN-yo

v = like the English b, but a little softer

x = like the English s except when it is between two vowels, then it is an "h" sound, so *oxicanto* is oh-hee-CAN-toh

z = like the English s in so, so *azul* (blue) is AH-sool

c and **g** are tricky because they each have two pronunciations:

c with **e** or **i** has an s sound, so *lúcida* (lucid or clear) is LOO-see-dah; but **c** with **a**, **o**, or **u** is hard, like **k**, so *buscar* (to look for) is BOOS-kar

g with **e** or **i** has an **h** sound, but **g** with **a**, **o**, or **u** is hard, like the English **g** in gut, so *fragil* (fragile) is frah-HEEL, but *siga* (to follow) is SEE-gah

ACCENT MARKS

The other thing you need to know to pronounce Spanish perfectly is how to read accent marks. You may have noticed that some words have little marks above one vowel. Unlike in some other languages (French for example), these marks do not change the way the vowel is pronounced, but they do change the stress of the word. That means they change which part of the word is said the strongest.

The general rule of stress in Spanish is that if there are two or more syllables (separate sounds), then the second to last one is stressed. Sometimes, however, this is not true so they use the stress marks to tell the reader that the stress is different in this word. For example, the words *fragíl* and *pájaro* have stress marks to show that the second to last syllable is NOT stressed in these words. *Fragíl* is frah-HEEL and *pájaro* is PAH-hah-row, not FRAH-heel and pah-HAH-row as they would be pronounced if they had no stress marks.

This all sounds very complicated, but once you practice a little, you will find Spanish is very easy to speak and musical to listen to. Here is a poem by one of Uruguay's most famous poets, Juana de Ibarbourou, about a palm tree. Using the rules above, practice saying the lines from the poem.

Soneto a Una Palma

Ya sin hambre ni sed, apenas alma
Apenas cuerpo que se va durmiendo;
Toda lúcida mente es como entiendo
La Infinitud de Dios en esta palma.

Cuando todo se vuelva eterna calma
Y siga el mar la fragíl tierra hendiendo
Poco a poco mi espiritú, volviendo
Irá a buscar morada en esta palma

Tal vez pequeño pájaro de canto
O humilde y tierno ramo de oxicanto
Con una flor azul junto a su planta
Mi palma ya será me patria eterna
Y ha de tener por siempre una lucerna:
La luz de una amistad que siembra y canta.

Sonnet to a Palm

Without hunger or thirst, hardly a soul
Hardly a body that goes to sleep;
All lucid mind is how I understand
The Infinity of God in this palm.

When all returns to the eternal calm
And the sea returns to flood the fragile earth
Little by little my spirit, returning
Will go to look for shelter in this palm

Maybe as a small bird of song
Or humble and tender branch of morning glory
With a blue flower next to its plant
My palm will be my eternal homeland
And there always has to be a grand light:
The light of a friendship that plants and sings.

ARTS

URUGUAY HAS A VERY RICH artistic community and history. With a traditionally high level of education and popular support for the arts, many varieties of creative pursuit have flourished in this tiny republic. Some examples of these pursuits are described in this chapter.

PERFORMING ARTS

Performing arts include music, theater, and dance. As a well-educated, largely urban people, Uruguayans have a rich and varied tradition of performing arts. Most of this is centered in Montevideo, but even department capitals and towns often support local theater and musicians.

Left: **A festive scene of students dancing and playing music in one of the main streets of Montevideo.**

Opposite: **Paintings from a street artist in Montevideo.**

THEATER The Teatro Solís (Solís Theater) in Montevideo is the home of the National Comedy Repertory Company. This group of actors and directors regularly performs new and old works by Latin American playwrights.

The most famous of Uruguayan playwrights is Florencio Sánchez. He was born in 1875 and wrote plays set in the Río de la Plata region. His characters are usually Uruguayan, Argentinian, or Paraguayan and tend to come from the working class. His plays are famous for their realistic dialogue and insightful portrayal of life in the slums of Buenos Aires or Montevideo. Some of his plays feature the conflict between rural living and the modern changes introduced from the cities. Sánchez has been compared to famous playwrights like Dostoevsky and Gorky.

One modern playwright is Mauricio Rosencof. He began writing in the 1960s but then decided to join the Tupamaros in their fight against the government. He was arrested and jailed for over 10 years. Whenever he was allowed to have paper, he continued to write poetry in jail, mostly about what it felt like to be tortured and imprisoned. He was released in 1985 along with other Tupamaros.

Other theaters in Montevideo include the Odeon Theater, which features Shakespeare along with modern dramas, and the Verdi Theater, which produces mostly comedies. Both universities and many secondary schools around the country support amateur theater groups.

MUSIC AS POLITICS

Uruguayans have always used musical forms to comment on everyday life and politics. Since the early days of independence, songwriters have been using music to tell stories about the civil wars between the Colorados and Blancos and to make fun of their enemies. In more recent times, three song forms have become the favored media for political criticism: Carnival *murgas* ("MOOR-gahs"), the tango, and the *canto popular* ("KAHN-toh poh-poo-LAHR").

Murgas are written to be sung as part of street theater productions that take place in every neighborhood during Carnival. These songs frequently focus on some politician or political event from the past year.

Tango songs are usually about the conflicts between men and women, especially of the lower classes. In talking about relationships, they also describe the life of the urban poor and new immigrants. In this sense, the tango is a kind of social commentary about life on the streets.

Canto popular (popular song) started in the late 1960s when young musicians all over Latin America began to write songs about social problems and politics. They criticized their country's government and wanted to see changes in their country. In Uruguay, *canto popular* was heavily censored by the military, and many musicians were arrested or forced to leave the country. Some continued to try to make their messages heard through informal concerts and black market recordings. They were the only voice of the people under the systems of repression built by the army and police.

Uruguayans have always supported the right to free speech and open discussion of social and political problems. This tradition is nowhere more obvious than in the many forms of music that have reflected popular opinion over the 19th and 20th centuries.

DANCE AND MUSIC Perhaps the best-known music from this part of the
world is the tango. The tango is usually associated with Buenos Aires, but
as Buenos Aires and Montevideo are culturally almost indistinguishable,
the tango has developed in both places. The tango originated in the poor
slums on the outskirts of Buenos Aires in the 1880s. It is both a type of
dance and a special kind of music. A standard tango band has to include
six players: two *bandoneons* ("ban-doh-NAY-ons," a type of accordion
made in Germany), two violins, a piano, and a double bass. At first the
tango was just music and a form of intimate dance for men and women.
Then in the 1920s, the lyrics became just as important as the music and the
dance. The lyrics tended to have sad themes like break-ups between men
and women and street life for the poor. Tango clubs opened all over
Montevideo and Buenos Aires and artists made a living by selling records

and giving live performances. The most famous tango ever, *La Cumparsita,* was written by an Uruguayan named Gerardo H. Matos Rodríguez.

Another popular art form is the *candombe*, which originated in the African-Uruguayan community. *Candombe* refers to both the music and the dance. The music is distinctive as it uses special African drums called *tamborils* ("tahm-BOR-eels"). *Candombe* music and dance are part of two festivals celebrated in Montevideo.

Uruguay has produced two classical composers: Eduardo Fabini and Héctor Errecart. Fabini is famous for his symphonies, while Errecart adapted traditional gaucho music to a classical form. His use of folk music themes has made him world-renowned.

There is a National School of Ballet in Uruguay, and although there is no opera company, stars performing in Buenos Aires will often stop in Montevideo too.

PEDRO FIGARI

Figari was born in Montevideo in 1861. He had no formal art training as a boy, though in 1886 he did go to Venice to study with an artist there named Virgilio Ripari. His real career as a painter did not start until 1921, when he was 60 years old and had his first exhibition in Buenos Aires.

His favorite themes were scenes of rural life showing gauchos, African-Uruguayans, country women, landscapes, and horses. His work is praised for his use of brush strokes and color to portray movement and light. Figari's landscapes are among the few that capture the special light of sunset on the open grasslands. In his work, he tried to preserve life in the countryside in the 19th century as he remembered it. He also wanted to show that African-Uruguayans had made an important contribution to Uruguayan life. Some of his more well-known works show scenes of *candombes* (African-Uruguayan festivals) and parties.

In 1925 he went to Paris where he perfected his painting style and lived for 12 years. In 1930 he won two awards for his art, one from Uruguay and one in Seville, Spain, at an international competition. He was a founding member of Uruguay's School of Arts in 1898 and was also a member of the Friends of Art in Buenos Aires. Though his painting career was late to start and short-lived (he died in 1938), Figari produced over 3,000 paintings. These are some of the images of the 19th century countryside that remain to remind Uruguayans of their heritage.

VISUAL ARTS

Uruguay has a long tradition of supporting the visual arts and has produced some important artists. The most famous is Pedro Figari, who is profiled on page 89. Another artist who tried to capture rural living in his work is Carlos Gonzalez. He is not a painter; rather he makes prints using wood blocks. These are called woodcuts and are made by carving the picture into a block of wood, then inking the wood and pressing it onto paper. Gonzalez' work portrays old-fashioned rural living and focuses especially on gaucho culture. Many of his woodcuts show gauchos in typical scenes: huddled over a campfire for warmth at night or sharing some *mate* on the plains. Gonzalez' style is called primitivism because he uses very simple lines and carves only with a knife. This makes his work appear a little rough, much like his subjects.

Right: **La Carreta,** part of a sculpture in Montevideo by José Belloni honoring the first pioneers.

Opposite: **Statue of the Gaucho,** a sculpture by José Luis Zorilla de San Martín.

In Montevideo's parks, you can see some examples of Uruguayan sculpture. Perhaps the most photographed of all is the sculpture of the covered wagon or *carreta* ("car-RAY-tah") being pulled by three oxen and driven by a bearded man. This represents the pioneers who first left the shores of the Río de la Plata to settle the interior of the country. The sculpture is by José Belloni and stands in Batlle Park.

The second most famous sculpture is the gaucho on his horse that stands at the intersection of two large streets in downtown Montevideo. This was made by José Luis Zorilla de San Martín, son of a famous writer.

LITERARY ARTS

This is the area of artistic endeavor in which Uruguay has excelled. Once again, as a result of a high literacy rate and a commitment to freedom of speech, Uruguayans have turned more to writing to express themselves than to any other art form. Many early works focused on nationalistic themes and on the rural heritage of the country.

Juan Zorilla de San Martín, father of sculptor José Luis, was both a poet and a diplomat. In 1879 he wrote the poem *The Patriotic Legend* in honor of Uruguay's history. His other famous

The beginning of the literary explosion in Uruguay came at the end of the 19th century. As open conflict between political factions declined, people began to consider what it meant to be Uruguayan.

SHAKESPEARE IN URUGUAY

Probably the most influential book ever written by an Uruguayan is *Ariel* by José Enrique Rodó. It was written in 1900 when Rodó was only 29. The book is actually a speech given by a fictitious teacher to his students. The students call the teacher Prospero because he keeps a big statue of Ariel in his study.

These are characters from William Shakespeare's play *The Tempest*. In *The Tempest*, the main character is a magician, Prospero, who lives alone on an island with his daughter and a savage, Caliban. Prospero's magic comes from a beautiful spirit he controls named Ariel. Ariel represents light and virtue whereas Caliban represents greed and basic needs. Shakespeare's play serves as the symbol used by the teacher to tell his students how they should live life. He says they should try to develop all their human qualities, not just the ones that satisfy basic needs like hunger and thirst. In other words, they should be more like Ariel than Caliban.

Rodó's book suggested that the US model of development was materialistic, like Caliban, whereas Latin American development should be idealistic, like Ariel. This was one of the most significant early efforts by Latin American thinkers to define the difference between the South and the North.

poem is the epic *Tabaré*. It is a long adventure story about the Charrúa Indians and is read throughout southern Latin America. Zorilla also started a public newspaper in 1878 and served as Uruguay's ambassador to the Vatican, France, and Spain.

Javier de Viana wrote about the end of the gaucho era. He captured the poverty and tragedy of gaucho life in his novel, *Gaucha*. He has been compared to a famous French writer, Emile Zola, who also wrote about downtrodden people. Eduardo Acevedo Díaz also portrayed gaucho life in his book *Soledad* (Solitude), published in 1894, but in a more positive way.

Luis Carlos Benvenuto is a historian whose work makes Uruguay's history understandable to everyone. His *Brief History of Uruguay*, published in the 1960s, shows how and why Uruguay had been rich but had stopped using its resources wisely.

Another nonfiction writer, Carlos Maggi, is a humorist who likes to poke fun at Uruguayan culture and history. He especially makes fun of Uruguayans who worship the gaucho past and the legends of the tango era. He has also written a movie, *The Yellow Ray,* which won a prize at the International Film Festival at Brussels.

A newsstand selling the popular dailies, *Búsqueda* and *Brecha*.

Before censorship shut down many newspapers and journals, Uruguay had a thriving tradition of literary criticism. The monthly magazine *La Marcha* was read far beyond Montevideo because of its high standard of writing and criticism. Many young writers including Eduardo Galeano got their start publishing stories in *La Marcha*.

The military closed *La Marcha* because it was too left-wing. Since 1985 another journal, *Brecha,* has been published. It is good but not as good as its predecessor because many talented writers and editors have left the country. Likewise with newspapers, many were forced to close during the dictatorship but have since reopened. With a return to a stable democracy, there are sure to be many more generations of great Uruguayan writers.

Most dailies are associated with a particular political group and will report the news according to their way of looking at things. No single newspaper is absolutely objective, but since everyone has access to more than one newspaper, one can easily get a balanced view by reading different opinions. The best modern newspaper is the weekly *Búsqueda.*

JUANA DE AMERICA

Juana de Ibarbourou is Uruguay's best-loved female poet. She was born in Melo in 1892 and started publishing her poetry in 1918 when she moved to Montevideo. In her early life, she wrote and published a lot and became quite popular both within and outside of Uruguay. In 1929, she was nicknamed *Juana de America* (Juana of America) in a public ceremony in her honor at the National University.

Throughout her life, she faced many tragedies including the deaths of her parents and of her husband. These events are reflected in her poetry, which is sometimes very sad and religious. The theme of death is part of her *Sonnet to a Palm* found on page 83. This poem resulted in a palm tree in Montevideo being dedicated to her. It was planted in the same spot as the original palm tree that she could see from her house and that had inspired her poem.

In 1947 she was elected to the Academy of Fine Arts. In 1957 she was honored by UNESCO in a special meeting in her honor. Her works have all been reprinted many times and some have been translated into English. Sadly, she died poor and nearly forgotten in Montevideo in 1979. Ironically, once she died, the public remembered her contribution to art and she was given a state funeral complete with a flag on her coffin.

FOLK CULTURE

Folk culture or folk art refers to the culture and art of the common people. In this category falls much of the art of rural Uruguay. One particularly special type of folk craft is the *mate* cup and straw. Traditionally, *mate* was drunk from a hollowed-out gourd that was often decorated with silver and had a silver top. To drink out of the gourd, one used a silver straw called a *bombilla* that was usually carved in beautiful patterns. This would have been one of the prized possessions of any Uruguayan fortunate enough to be able to buy one. Nowadays, these items have been replaced with cheaper cups and straws, but older versions can be seen proudly displayed in the homes of Uruguayans.

A more modern form of craft is the handknit sweater. These bright and colorful items of clothing are made by women working in their homes. They are heavy and warm, and each one is unique. Knitting is an important source of income for poorer women in the countryside and in the cities.

You can sometimes buy authentic antique gourds and *bombillas* from the sidewalk markets in Montevideo.

LEISURE

THERE ARE A WIDE VARIETY OF ACTIVITIES for Uruguayans to enjoy in their leisure time. They participate in a number of sports and pastimes. Some of their leisure time is spent in ways similar to people in other countries, and some is spent in distinctly Uruguayan fashion.

SPORTS

SOCCER The most popular sport in the country is soccer. Every able-bodied boy in Uruguay has played soccer at school or in local fields, and everyone follows their favorite team. On July 18, 1930, the first World Cup soccer finals were held in Montevideo's Centenary Stadium and Uruguay was one of the competing teams. Uruguay won the championship and the celebrations that resulted from that win are still remembered as the loudest and wildest in the history of the country.

Left: **It cannot be emphasized strongly enough that soccer is the one thing that unites the whole country; everyone watches and almost every Uruguayan male plays at some point in his life.**

Opposite: **A girl relaxes on one of the benches in a park in Montevideo.**

With satellite television, Uruguayans are beginning to pick up American sports like basketball and baseball, but the sports that have the longest traditions are those from England like polo and soccer.

OTHER SPORTS AND COMPETITIONS With so many beaches lining the Río de la Plata between Montevideo and Punta del Este, water sports are very common in Uruguay. There are many boat races, both for motorboats and sailboats. There is an annual international competition of Formula 1 race boats, and participants in the Whitbread Sailboat Race stop in Uruguay. During the summer, windsurfing competitions attract international competitors. Swimming is very popular, both as a sport and as recreation. Every year there is a swimming race in the Punta del Este area, to the east of Montevideo.

Another race that attracts local and international attention is the annual Grand Prix car race, also in Punta del Este. For people with simpler tastes, there is the San Fernando Marathon. Besides water sports, Uruguayans enjoy basketball, tennis, polo, and golf. There are also competitions to show purebred Arabian horses, which are the pride of Uruguay.

LEISURE ACTIVITIES

CINEMA One of the most popular forms of entertainment is the cinema. There are movie theaters all over the country. A small local film industry and foreign films provide entertainment variety. In larger urban centers, there is often a lively theater scene. In Montevideo, the population is large enough to attract international shows that tour the world.

NIGHTLIFE Nightlife includes *peñas* ("PAYN-yahs") or clubs with live music. While the *peñas* tend to be popular with the young, older people are more likely to go to old-fashioned tango bars to hear live music. For those with a sense of adventure, there are also clubs specializing in *candombe* or African-Uruguayan music. Other musical tastes are catered to by the symphony and the occasional opera in Montevideo.

For people on a limited budget, nightlife might include a stroll around the downtown area and a stop in one of Montevideo's many cafés and late-night restaurants. Other types of leisure activities include gambling at one of the two government-owned casinos in Montevideo, Casino del Parque Rodó and the Hotel Carrasco Casino.

STROLLING Part of the Spanish heritage in Uruguayan culture is a love of strolling. It may not sound like much in the way of entertainment, but there is a tradition of going for walks with family and friends. In addition to the shopping districts, Montevideo has many public parks and gardens well-suited to this purpose. Ideally, a stroll finishes with a coffee, ice cream, or *mate* with friends.

Above: **Nightlife includes going out with friends and eating in a restaurant like this one in the city center of Punta del Este.**

Opposite: **Uruguayans and tourists alike enjoy the beautiful beaches and the exciting water sports available in Uruguay.**

99

SHOPPING Window shopping is also very popular. The main shopping street in Montevideo is 18th of July Avenue, which boasts boutiques from all over the world. Recently, Montevideo has also promoted North American-style shopping malls, and there are now four in the city. Two are architecturally quite distinctive: Punta Carretas, a renovated prison, and Barrio Reus, located in a formerly poor area of the city. Architectural students renovated this area by painting all the old tenement buildings in bright colors, turning it into a tourist attraction today.

On the weekends there are street markets or *ferías* ("fay-REE-ahs"), which sell everything from junk to priceless antiques. They also sell food items such as vegetables and sausages.

Walking around in an open-air flea market is a favorite Uruguayan pastime.

VACATION TIME

During the summer (December to March), most Uruguayans living in or near Montevideo will spend their spare time at one of the many beaches strung out along the drive from Montevideo to Punta del Este. Those with limited budgets will either just go for the day or will look for economical cottages to rent. Those with more money to spend have villas or can afford to rent homes in Punta del Este for the two-month summer vacation. Wherever they end up, however, summer time will be family barbecue time. Every rental house and villa has its own wood-fired barbecue, and the most popular summer food is grilled meat.

PUNTA DEL ESTE Punta del Este is the main tourist resort in the country. When it is open during the summer, it is the place to be in Uruguay. Located to the east of Montevideo, Punta del Este has a 25-mile (40 km) stretch of beach. Its beauty is comparable to the resort areas of the French Riviera. Throughout the season, there are many sport competitions and activities for singles and families. It is as if the cultural center of Uruguay shifts for the summer season from Montevideo to Punta del Este. There are open-air concerts, theater performances and premieres, dance performances and recitals. These are held at one of the two big clubs: Club del Lago or the Cantegril.

There are also local-level sport competitions and beauty contests to keep young people busy. The season ends with the Festival of the Sea. After that, everyone packs up and goes home for another 10 months of city living.

Teenage girls walking on the Punta del Este beach. People tend to get up late, have fun on the beach until late afternoon, go home for a long nap and get up again around 9 or 10 at night to enjoy the nightlife until dawn.

PIRIAPOLIS Piriapolis, to the east of Montevideo, was Uruguay's first seaside resort. It was built in the 1920s by Francisco Piria, who founded the landmark Argentino Hotel. Piriapolis is still an active resort town, but it is much quieter than Punta del Este. This resort attracts people who want a more healthful vacation than the wild nights Punta del Este provides. Recently, thermal baths using warmed ocean water have been built. People now go to Piriapolis for the health and beauty spa.

OTHER DESTINATIONS Uruguayans who prefer something different can go to the interior of the country for a vacation. Some popular destinations include the thermal springs near Salto and Paysandú in the northwest. These springs result from warm water bubbling to the surface, creating pools. Family resorts have been built around the springs, with hotels, movie theaters, shopping areas, and restaurants.

For those interested in nature, there is the department of Rocha in the southeast. Here the coast is much rockier and, being on the Atlantic Ocean, the water is rougher. Small fishing villages are scattered along the coast, and the rocks support a large colony of sea lions. Fishing enthusiasts find boats for hire and nature lovers enjoy the wilder feel of this remote area.

Inland, there are parks and nature reserves that are home to Uruguay's wildlife. Some of these parks permit hunting and fishing with a license, while others are for observation only.

People also enjoy taking country drives throughout the year to see the fantastic scenery of the plains. Some of the old ranch houses are open for guests as bed-and-breakfast places.

For those who want a quiet vacation away from the noise of Punta del Este, fishing in Maldonado is an alternative.

FESTIVALS

URUGUAY CELEBRATES both religious and secular holidays drawn from its history. This chapter looks at what Uruguayans consider to be their most important festivals.

EPIPHANY

In many Catholic countries this day is as important as Christmas because it is the day when the Three Kings visited Jesus and brought him gifts. In Uruguay, this day has become an African-Uruguayan celebration. Black slaves were not as segregated from Whites during the colonial period. They generally were close to the families they worked for. As a result, they became Catholics and celebrated Epiphany as the day when the Black king, Saint Balthasar, visited Jesus.

Left: **African-Uruguayans celebrate Epiphany and Carnival with colorful costumes and dancing in the streets.**

Opposite: **A** *bandoneon* **player usually provides music for the gaucho dance.**

CALENDAR OF FESTIVALS AND IMPORTANT DAYS

Uruguayans are not very religious. For that reason, some of the traditional Christian celebrations have different, non-religious names. For example, Easter Week is called Semana Criolla or Tourism Week and Christmas is called Family Day. Many of the other public holidays are celebrations of important moments in Uruguayan history.

January 1:	New Year's Day
January 6:	Epiphany, Day of Saint Balthasar
February:	Carnival
March/April:	Semana Criolla or Tourism Week (Easter Week)
March/April:	Fiesta del Mar, Festival of the Sea
April 19:	Landing of the Immortal 33
May 1:	Labor Day
May 18:	Day of the Battle of Las Piedras
June 19:	Birthday of General Artigas
July 18:	Constitution Day
August 25:	Independence Day
October 12:	Discovery of America, also known as Día de la Raza or Day of Race
November 2:	All Souls' Day
December 8:	Beach Day
December 25:	Family Day (Christmas)

Most Blacks lived in Montevideo throughout the colonial period and 19th century. At that time, they organized themselves into groups called nations based on their area of origin in Africa. These nations were mutual aid societies, which means that members would help each other in times of need. Each nation would also sponsor its own dance and parade group. Periodically through the year, the nations would organize a dance celebration known as a *candombe*. Each nation elected a king and queen for that *candombe*; they would then compete with other kings and queens to be judged the best dancers.

On Epiphany, January 6, African-Uruguayans of Montevideo organize a large *candombe* celebration. They parade through the city playing their music and dancing in their nation groups.

CARNIVAL

Carnival is linked to the Catholic custom of Lent, the 40 days before Easter when practicing Catholics give up eating meat to show respect for the death of Christ on Good Friday. Carnival takes place three days to a week before Lent begins. It is everyone's last chance to feast and celebrate before the serious time of Lent begins.

Carnival has been celebrated in Europe since the Middle Ages. The name comes from the Latin *carne vale*, which means "farewell to meat." Carnival has a long tradition in the New World and has been celebrated in Montevideo since the earliest colonial times.

The modern Carnival in Uruguay lasts three days. During this time, there are parades of dancers and decorated floats through the streets. The African-Uruguayan community is famous for the dance groups it sends to these parades. A Queen of Carnival is elected as the most beautiful girl in Montevideo and she has two vice-queens in her court. There are light shows in the streets and a general atmosphere of festivity.

Participants in the street theater called *tablada* ("tah-BLAH-dah") during Carnival celebrations perform their special songs called *murgas*.

One distinctive feature of the Montevideo Carnival is the street theater or *tablada*. Every neighborhood community will collect money during the year in order to put on a play for the Carnival. They build huge stages on street corners and hire writers and directors to create a play in which the local people will act. Different communities compete with one another to put on the best *tablada* and will spend a lot of money to make their play the most spectacular, with lights and set decoration. The plays are pure fantasy or romance, but sometimes they make fun of local politicians or international stars. Musicians also create special songs for the *tabladas*. These are called *murgas* and often have a political or humorous side to them.

Although Carnival officially lasts three days, the dancers and theater groups continue to perform in public parks and hotels for up to a month. So much planning is involved in these productions that the organizers want everyone to be able to enjoy their efforts for longer than the official public holiday permits.

SEMANA CRIOLLA OR TOURISM WEEK

In place of the religious celebrations of Easter, Uruguayans prefer to remember their own cultural past. *Semana Criolla* or Creole Week is named after the first descendants of Europeans born in the New World, called creoles or *criollos* ("kree-OHL-yohs") in Spanish. The main idea of the week is to remember and celebrate the gauchos. Men wear typical gaucho clothes and paraphernalia and take part in various contests of gaucho skills including riding bulls, breaking horses, and trick riding.

Only 30 men are allowed to compete and they are carefully chosen from applicants from all over the country. They can win prizes for the best costume, riding equipment, dancing, singing, lassoing, and bronco-busting. Women can also compete; Uruguayans still remember a woman named Nieves Mira who was very beautiful and talented.

Another famous gaucho was "El Fantasma," or The Ghost. He was an African-Uruguayan who did all his tricks with his poncho over his eyes! These events are quite spectacular and many tourists come to Montevideo to see the competitions. This is why Semana Criolla is also sometimes called Tourism Week.

FIESTA DEL MAR OR FESTIVAL OF THE SEA

This takes place at the end of the southern summer, around March or April. The beach between Punta del Este and Punta Ballena is brightly lit with lights. The first part of the celebration is a parade of decorated boats. In the evening, a Queen of the Sea is crowned at one of the social clubs.

The contestants for the title wait for a man dressed as the Roman sea god Neptune to emerge from the water. He will approach the winner and place a special crown on her head. She will then be paraded through Punta del Este with a long line of cars behind her float. The celebration ends with an hour-long fireworks display. This officially ends the summer.

Honda Beach during the festivities becomes the place to be for meeting people, dancing, drinking, and having fun.

BEACH DAY

Uruguay is south of the equator and so the seasons are reversed. December 8 is the official opening of the beaches and the beginning of the summer vacation for Uruguayans. Before anyone enters the ocean, a priest blesses the waters to make them safe. There are also regattas or sailing competitions at various ports. In Carrasco, there is an international shooting competition.

HISTORICAL HOLIDAYS

The most important of the national holidays is Independence Day on August 25 when ceremonies are held in Independence Square in Montevideo. Constitution Day on July 18 celebrates the first constitution drafted and signed in 1830. Finally, April 19 is the day when everyone remembers the landing of the Immortal 33 in Montevideo to try to free Uruguay from the Brazilians. All of these days are public holidays and times to display great patriotism.

Two days are devoted to the memory of José Artigas. One is on June 19, which commemorates his birthday. The other is May 18, which celebrates his famous victory at the Battle of Las Piedras. Las Piedras is a village not far from Montevideo where, in 1811, Artigas and his small band of soldiers confronted the Spanish loyalists. After six hours of fighting, Artigas was victorious.

The battle is not significant because of the number of Spanish losses or the scale of the victory but because it gave people hope that the Spaniards could be beaten. As a result of this victory, Artigas was able to rally a large force of men when he marched out of Montevideo. This was the event that made Artigas famous as "The Chief of the Orientals," as Uruguayans were then called.

Politicians and other important people make speeches on Independence Day about the courageous struggle for independence that was fought first against the Spanish and then against the Brazilians.

111

FOOD

URUGUAYAN CUISINE is the result of many influences including gaucho, Spanish, and Italian. When all of these are combined, the result is delicious. This chapter introduces some Uruguayan foods and provides a recipe for a favorite meal.

TYPICAL FOODS AND BEVERAGES

The central part of all main meals in Uruguay is meat. In the early days of independence and trade with Britain, the main export was not meat, but hides. This was because there was no easy way to ship meat in the days before refrigeration. Late in the 19th century, canning technology was developed and meat was then exported to Europe, but previously the gauchos rounded up animals for slaughter and were left with literally tons of meat once the hides were removed. Meat thus became the basis of the Uruguayan diet.

Left: **A gaucho speciality is *asados con cuero*, or cooking a whole animal in its skin. This preserves the fat and juices and makes the meat very tender. This type of meal is still served in speciality restaurants and on special occasions when many people gather together.**

Opposite: **Sausages are a staple in the Uruguayan diet.**

The barbecue or *parillada* ("pah-reel-YAH-dah") is the most popular way to cook meat. All Uruguayan homes have an outdoor grill for this purpose. They use wood or wood charcoal to cook with rather than gas because it gives the meat added flavor. Meat is also processed into other forms. A favorite is *moncilla* ("mone-SEEL-yah"), a blood sausage. Meat may also be used in *empanadas* ("aym-pah-NAH-dahs") or pastry turnovers. *Chivitos* ("chee-VEE-tohs") are a kind of local fast-food sandwich that usually includes egg, tomato, thinly sliced steak, cheese, and lettuce piled high in a bun. Other fast foods using meat are *olímpicos* ("oh-LEEM-pee-kohs"), *húngaros* ("OON-gah-rohs"), and *panchos* ("PAHN-chohs," hot dogs). *Olímpicos* are essentially club sandwiches. *Húngaros* and *panchos* are both sausages served on buns like hot dogs, but *húngaros* are very spicy. A country favorite is the meat stew or *estofado* ("ay-stoh-FAH-doh"). It originated on the open plains and is very hearty.

The *parillada* or barbecue is very popular. A variety of meats are cooked here, including different kinds of sausages, beef, and chicken.

A typical family meal includes meat as the central dish (usually beef or chicken) with potatoes, bread, and a green salad. Potatoes are the essential accompaniment to huge slabs of steak.

With the large numbers of Italian immigrants in the 20th century, Uruguay's diet has been supplemented with other foods. Some of the first businesses opened by Italians were pasta-making factories. They also imported their favorite foods such as parmesan cheese and prosciutto ham (dried ham). As these became popular in pasta and pizza dishes, Uruguayans began producing their own. Typical Italian-Uruguayan pizza is made in a wood-burning oven in keeping with the barbecue tradition.

The Spanish heritage can be seen in the way seafood and stews are cooked. Many local dishes feature mussels, shrimps, and cockles along with freshwater and saltwater fish. Along the coast, restaurants offer freshly caught fish and shellfish.

Desserts have also been influenced by Uruguay's European heritage. Pastry was brought by the Italian immigrants, and most cafés feature delicious examples. The Spanish influence on desserts can be seen in the frequent use of *dulce de leche* ("DOOL-say day LAY-chay," literally sweetness of milk), a kind of thick, concentrated sweetened milk. Dulce is used as a sauce with fruit or spread on bread and pastry. It is incredibly sweet and rich.

In Uruguay, as in the rest of Latin America, the large supermarket is still not the norm for shopping. People prefer to buy their food from shops specializing in particular products. If you want the freshest vegetables, you go to the grocer, for meat you visit your local butcher, for fish the fishmonger, and so on.

The other reason for this type of shopping is that most working-class and middle-class people do not have the space to store food for a long time. They do their shopping every day or every couple of days and do not tend to freeze food for later use.

The drink of choice throughout the day is *mate*, a tea made with the leaves of the *yerba mate*, which is native to South America. Europeans learned to drink *mate* from the indigenous peoples. *Mate* contains quite a lot of caffeine and is a little like coffee in North American culture. Uruguayans drink so much *mate*, many of them carry a thermos of hot water everywhere they go so they can prepare fresh cups of the drink.

Uruguay also produces its own beer and wine. One particularly Uruguayan drink is *clericó* ("klay-ree-KOH"), which is a mixture of white wine and fruit juice. Sparkling wine mixed with white wine is called *medio y medio* ("MAY-dee-oh ee MAY-dee-oh") or "half and half."

MATE

Yerba mate is a relative of the European holly tree. Its leaves are harvested and dried. To make *mate*, you pack a cup or *mate* gourd full of the leaves and then add hot water. This mixture is left to steep. When the water is infused with the flavor of the *mate*, a straw or *bombilla* is slipped into the container full of leaves, and the liquid is drunk through it. *Mate* is quite bitter and is an acquired taste.

Social importance is attached to *mate* drinking. Among indigenous peoples *mate* drinking was done in small groups, with the cup passed around for everyone to enjoy. The first Europeans to develop this social habit were the gauchos who would gather together in small groups in the evenings. Not only do people like to drink it all day, but as much as possible they gather together to share the drink.

Interestingly, during the military dictatorship, when most forms of public meeting were prohibited, *mate* gatherings became one of the few ways people could legally meet and talk with one another. Those wanting to pass information, or just be together in larger groups, gathered at local *mate* snack shops. Since there was nothing particularly political about this, the police and army ignored it.

Mate *is far more than a drink for Uruguayans. It represents their past and the heritage of indigenous cultures. It also continues to serve as a kind of social glue that gathers people together throughout the day for a chat and a sip.*

MEALTIMES

The Uruguayan pattern of eating is quite similar to that found in southern Europe. Breakfast for many Uruguayans is a cup of coffee or *mate* and a large croissant. They return for a long lunch break, often lasting from 12 or 1 p.m. to 3 or 4 p.m.

Lunch is the main meal of the day. This usually includes a first course such as a salad or soup, a main course of meat and vegetables, and dessert. Since this meal is the heaviest of the day, people often take a nap afterwards to help with digestion; then they return to work until 7 or 8 p.m. Late in the evening, they will have a second, lighter meal. This may not be eaten until 10 or 11 at night, which is not very late if one remembers that they have taken a nap at midday.

People eating at a restaurant in the Port Market of Montevideo. The Uruguayan's biggest meal is lunch. This is usually followed by a nap or *siesta*.

EATING OUT

Eating out is very popular in the cities. Montevideo offers every type of restaurant and price range imaginable, and restaurants are open morning, noon, and night. In the mornings, cafés everywhere serve coffee and light breakfasts for people on their way to work.

At mid-morning, many workers take a short break from work and gather in cafeterias for some *mate* or coffee and a chat with co-workers. These corner snack bars are great for mixing all types of people. It is not unusual for blue-collar workers, secretaries, and business people to go to the same snack bar.

People who cannot get home for lunch will go to a restaurant near their work place or school. Many restaurants cater to those eating out with something called the fixed, three-course menu of the day—a set meal that does not allow customers to choose what they want. The advantage for the restaurant is that there is no need to stock many different foods; for the customer, the fixed price menu is fairly cheap. People often have a favorite place to eat lunch and go there every day.

For the late evening meal, there are a variety of foods and styles of service. From Italian gourmet to pizza parlors, from pubs to fancy French restaurants—it is all in Montevideo and other big cities. The most popular type of restaurant is called a *parillada* (barbecue or grill). These places cater to the Uruguayan passion for grilled meat and use only wood charcoal.

Montevideo offers many options for the hearty eater, including gourmet Italian restaurants.

Tourists and Uruguayans enjoy dining at this gaucho tourist ranch. Some theme restaurants are practically museums to the gaucho way of life.

Another speciality restaurant is the gaucho club. These clubs are decorated with pictures and mementos of gaucho life. They specialize in gaucho food such as *asado con cuero* and *mazamorra* ("mah-zah-MOHR-rah") or ground corn with milk. For simpler tastes, there are *cervecerias* ("sayr-vay-say-REE-ahs") or beer gardens. Along with beer, they serve *chivitos* and other snack foods. But do not even think about eating until at least 10 at night or you might find that none of the restaurants are open.

Outside the biggest cities, there are fewer fancy restaurants and certainly no foreign food. In rural areas, distances are much greater and budgets much smaller, so people do not tend to eat out very much. The basis of the rural diet is still meat and potatoes, and people eat less fish, being farther from the coast. Another staple in the diet is rice. Uruguay is an exporter of rice and this staple is used as a cheap filler in stews.

ESTOFADO: BEEF STEW

fresh corn cut from 3 ears
1 pound (500 g) stewing beef, cut into cubes
1 teaspoon sugar
3 small summer squash, cut into large pieces
4 white potatoes, peeled and halved
4 sweet potatoes, peeled and cut into large pieces
4 carrots, scraped and cut into large sections
1 onion, chopped
1 green pepper, chopped
1 tablespoon minced parsley
a dash of paprika
2 tablespoons cooking oil
salt and pepper

Cut the corn from the ears and cook in salted, boiling water for a few minutes.

Sprinkle sugar on meat cubes and add meat to the corn. Simmer for 30 minutes.

Add squash, white potatoes, sweet potatoes, and carrots.

Cook over low heat until the mixture thickens (about 2 hours).

Sauté onion, green pepper, parsley, and paprika in the oil and add to the stew when the onions are soft. Season with salt and pepper to taste.

Serve and enjoy. There is enough for 4–6 people.

PARILLADA BARBECUE SAUCE

1 large onion, chopped
1 tomato, chopped
1 green pepper, chopped
2 cloves garlic, crushed
1 tablespoon finely chopped parsley
2 tablespoons olive oil
2 tablespoons vinegar

Cook everything together until the mixture is a thick sauce. Use it to coat barbecued beef after it is cooked and before serving.

In recent years, North Americans have been eating less red meat and smaller portions. Not so for the Uruguayans, who continue to appreciate one-pound cuts on their plates.

URUGUAY

Map Legend

- Capital city
- Major town
- Mountain peak

Feet	Meters
16,500	5,000
9,900	3,000
6,600	2,000
3,300	1,000
1,650	500
660	200
0	0

BRAZIL

ARGENTINA

ARTIGAS

Rivera

SALTO

Salto Grande

Salto

Cuchilla de Belén

Río Cuareim

Tacuarembó

RIVERA

Cuchilla de Haedo

PAYSANDÚ

TACUAREMBÓ

Paysandú

Río Uruguay

Melo

CERRO LARGO

Río Negro

RÍO NEGRO

Río Negro (Black River)

Río Yí

Black River Lake

Grande

Merín Lagoon

Fray Bentos

DURAZNO

Río Yí

TREINTA Y TRES

Mercedes

SORIANO

FLORES

FLORIDA

LAVALLEJA

Cuchilla Grande

ROCHA

COLONIA

SAN JOSÉ

Río Santa Lucía

Minas

Mt. Catedral (1,684ft / 513m)

Colonia

Canelones

CANELONES

MALDONADO

Las Piedras

Mt. Animas

MONTEVIDEO

Piriapolis

Buenos Aires

Río de la Plata (Silver River)

Isla de Lobos

Punta del Este

ATLANTIC

OCEAN

N

0	50	100 Miles
0	50	100	150 Kilometers

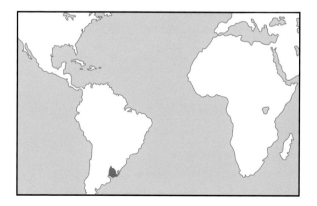

QUICK NOTES

OFFICIAL NAME
República Oriental del Uruguay
(Oriental Republic of Uruguay)

LAND AREA
68,020 square miles (176,220 square kilometers)

POPULATION
3.1 million

CAPITAL
Montevideo

DEPARTMENTS OR STATES
Artigas, Canelones, Cerro Largo, Colonia, Durazno, Flores, Florida, Lavalleja, Maldonado, Montevideo, Paysandú, Río Negro, Rivera, Rocha, Salto, San José, Soriano, Tacuarembó, Treinta y Tres

NATIONAL SYMBOL
Sun of May

NATIONAL FLAG
Nine horizontal stripes of blue and white with white canton containing Sun of May in gold

MAJOR RIVERS
Río de la Plata, Río Uruguay, Río Negro

MAJOR LAKE
Black River Lake

NATIONAL/OFFICIAL LANGUAGES
Spanish

HIGHEST POINT
Mount Catedral at 1,684 feet (513 meters)

LITERACY
96%

LIFE EXPECTANCY
70 years (men); 76 years (women)

MAJOR RELIGIONS
Catholic, Protestant

CURRENCY
Uruguayan peso (UYP)
US$1 = 10.315 Uruguayan pesos (May 1998)

MAIN EXPORTS
Beef, wool, leather, rice

IMPORTANT ANNIVERSARIES
April 19, Landing of the Immortal 33
June 19, Birthday of General Artigas
August 25, Independence Day

LEADERS IN POLITICS
José Gervasio Artigas, first nationalist to fight for independence
General Fructuoso Rivera, first president (1830–36)
José Batlle y Ordóñez, president (1903–07, and 1911–15)
Julio María Sanguinetti Cairolo, president, 1994–present

DISTINGUISHED WRITERS
José Enrique Rodó
Juana de Ibarbourou
Eduardo Galeano

GLOSSARY

Batllismo ("bahj-JEES-moh")
Government and social reform designed by José Batlle at the beginning of the 20th century.

boleadoras ("boh-lay-ah-DOR-ahs")
Weapon used by Charrúa Indians and gauchos to hunt animals, consisting of small rocks attached by leather thongs.

bombilla ("bohm-BEEL-ya")
Straw used to drink mate.

candombe ("can-DOHM-bay")
Music and dance of African-Uruguayan origin.

cocoliche ("ko-ko-LEE-chay")
A Spanish-Italian dialect spoken by first-generation Italian immigrants in Buenos Aires and Montevideo.

criollos ("kree-OHL-yohs")
Creoles, the first people of European descent born in the New World.

estancia ("ay-STAN-see-ah")
Large ranch.

fronterizo ("fron-tayr-EE-zoh")
Dialect that is a mix of Spanish and Portuguese spoken on the Brazilian-Uruguayan border.

Garra Charrúa ("GAR-rah char-ROO-ah")
Expression meaning brave, persistent, and fierce.

gaucho ("GOW-choh")
Traditional South American cowboy.

lunfardo ("loon-FAR-doh")
Working-class slang used in Buenos Aires and Montevideo.

mate ("MAH-tay")
Herbal drink.

MERCOSUR
The free trade agreement between Uruguay, Paraguay, Brazil, and Argentina that went into effect in 1995.

mestizo ("may-STEE-soh")
Person of mixed Spanish and Indian blood.

murga ("MOOR-gah")
Carnival song.

porteño ("por-TAYN-yoh")
A variety of Spanish spoken in Buenos Aires and Montevideo.

rastra ("RAHS-trah")
Wide belt made of metal worn by gauchos.

tablada ("tah-BLAH-dah")
Neighborhood street theater performed during Carnival.

Tupamaros ("too-pah-MAR-ohs")
Guerrilla fighters who challenged the government before the military dictatorship.

yerba mate ("YAYR-bah MAH-tay")
Plant whose leaves are used to make the Uruguayan tea called *mate*.

BIBLIOGRAPHY

Buckman, Robert T. *Latin America. The World Today Series.* West Virginia: Stryker-Post Publications: Harpers Ferry, 1997.

Coatsworth, Elizabeth. *Tales of the Gauchos: Stories by W.H. Hudson.* New York: Alfred A. Knopf, 1946.

Fisher, John R. *Latin America: From Conquest to Independence.* London: Rupert Hart-Davis, 1971.

Hudson, Rex A. and Sandra W. Meditz (editors). *Uruguay: A Country Study.* Area Handbook Series. Washington: Federal Research Division, Library of Congress. 1992.

McNaspy, C.J. *Lost Cities of Paraguay: Art and Architecture of the Jesuit Reductions, 1607–1767.* Chicago: Loyola University Press, 1982.

Morrison, Marion. *Let's Visit Uruguay.* Bridgeport, Connecticut: Burke Publishing Company, 1985.

Sosnowski, S. and L.B. Popkin (editors). *Repression, Exile and Democracy: Uruguayan Culture.* Series: Latin America in Translation. Durham: Duke University Press, 1993.

Tames, Richard. *The Conquest of South America.* London: Methuen, 1974.

Wilbert, Johannes and Karin Simoneau. *Folk Literature of the Makka Indians.* Los Angeles: UCLA Latin American Center Publications, 1991.

INDEX

INDEX